Bloom's Modern Critical Views

WILLIAM SHAKESPEARE: ROMANCES
New Edition

Edited and with an introduction by
Harold Bloom
Sterling Professor of the Humanities
Yale University

BLOOM'S
LITERARY CRITICISM
An imprint of Infobase Publishing

Bloom's Modern Critical Views: William Shakespeare: Romances—New Edition
Copyright © 2011 by Infobase Publishing
Introduction © 2011 by Harold Bloom

Bloom's Literary Criticism
An imprint of Infobase Publishing
132 West 31st Street
New York NY 10001

Library of Congress Cataloging-in-Publication Data
William Shakespeare. Romances / edited and with an introduction by Harold Bloom. — New ed.
  p. cm.—(Bloom's modern critical views)
 Includes bibliographical references and index.
 ISBN 978-1-60413-869-6 (hardcover)
 1. Shakespeare, William, 1564–1616—Tragicomedies. 2. Tragicomedy—History and criticism. I. Bloom, Harold.
 PR2981.5.W56 2010
 822.3'3—dc22

                              2010028993

Bloom's Literary Criticism books are available at special discounts when purchased in bulk quantities for businesses, associations, institutions, or sales promotions. Please call our Special Sales Department in New York at (212) 967-8800 or (800) 322-8755.

You can find Bloom's Literary Criticism on the World Wide Web at
http://www.chelseahouse.com

Contributing editor: Pamela Loos
Cover designed by Takeshi Takahashi
Composition by IBT Global, Troy NY
Cover printed by IBT Global, Troy NY
Book printed and bound by IBT Global, Troy NY
Date printed: November 2010
Printed in the United States of America

10 9 8 7 6 5 4 3 2 1

This book is printed on acid-free paper.

All links and Web addresses were checked and verified to be correct at the time of publication. Because of the dynamic nature of the Web, some addresses and links may have changed since publication and may no longer be valid.

Contents

Editor's Note

My introduction broods on the elements of obsession that perhaps bind these late Shakespearean plays together.

Northrop Frye sees in the romances and in *The Winter's Tale*, in particular, an embrace of spectacle and the primitive. Ruth Nevo speculates on genre complications as embodied by *Cymbeline* and its elements of the outlandish, coincidental, and grotesque.

René Girard turns his attention to the textual rehabilitation of Leontes in *The Winter's Tale*, after which Arthur Kirsch deepens our sense of the link between Montaigne and *The Tempest*.

Alan Stewart explores notions of friendship in *The Two Noble Kinsmen*, followed by W.H. Auden, who sees *Troilus and Cressida* as advancing and working out Shakespeare's stylistic challenges.

Richard Harp then analyzes the role of providence in the late plays. The volume concludes with Alexander Leggatt's view of *All's Well That Ends Well* as a shadow *Hamlet*, in the ways the former interweaves its preoccupations with comedy and death.

HAROLD BLOOM

Introduction

The Anglo-Irish critic Edward Dowden, a friend of the poet W.B. Yeats's family, created some long-range mischief when he first characterized a group of Shakespeare's final plays as "romances." Shakespeare, I suspect, thought of most of them as tragicomedies and may have regarded *The Tempest* as relatively unmixed comedy. But universal usage condemns us to call these visionary comedies *romances,* and so I will not argue the generic term here.

Most of the "romantic" features of *Cymbeline, The Winter's Tale, The Tempest,* and in the Shakespearean parts of *Pericles* and *The Two Noble Kinsmen* actually are more diverse than not and do not hold these five very different plays together as a group. While they are hardly Shakespeare's only studies in obsessive quests, that may be the common element in these late tragicomedies. Pericles mourns obsessively for his lost wife and daughter and, indeed, is traumatized before Marina restores him. Posthumus is almost more stupid than obsessive in his jealousy concerning Imogen, but he is insane enough to order her murdered. The cosmological fear of supposedly having been cuckolded is too titanic to be termed Leontes's obsession; a stronger term even than *madness* seems required.

Prospero, in *The Tempest,* might seem too wise a hermeticist, too much an anti-Faust to fit this pattern. And yet the deep scheme of his art has its compulsive strains; to win power over all his enemies, for whatever purpose, does not seem a wholly adequate project for a magus who tells us that he has raised the dead. Something obsessive urges Prospero on, though we cannot wholly grasp what that is.

1

In *The Two Noble Kinsmen,* Shakespeare ends his career with an extraordinary vision of erotic obsessiveness, so extreme that some revulsion from desire has to be argued as central to Shakespeare's share in the work. It seems odd that obsessiveness should be represented with different modes of authorial estrangement in these five late plays. *Pericles* (again, the Shakespearean acts 3 and 4) is a formal pageant, a kind of processional. *Cymbeline,* in my judgment, is partly a Shakespearean self-parody; many of his prior plays and characters are mocked by it. Perhaps *The Winter's Tale* is less a manifestation of the poet's detachment; there are more of Shakespeare's peculiar powers in it even than in *The Tempest,* but the conclusion, whether statue or long-hidden woman revives, seems to be an abatement of the pastoral ecstasy of Perdita's marvelous epiphany in act 4, scene 4. I myself go with Autolycus, for whom the play is a romantic comedy, rather than a romance.

Prospero's coldness, Ariel's nonhuman delicacy, and Caliban's half-human resentment (exalted by many these days as a heroic anticolonialism) do not render *The Tempest* less of a comedy, but they help augment our distance from what is represented onstage.

The Two Noble Kinsmen is almost its own genre, one that I cannot imagine sustaining any further development. Shakespeare's own stance in regard to it is a little uncanny; he has been repelled by Mars before and suffered from Venus, but both are dismissed here with a new completeness.

I have been suggesting that what holds the five "late romances" together (if they are so held at all) is a fresh stylization and formalized detachment in the representation of heightened conditions of obsession. Shakespeare's art certainly was not waning, but his interest in it probably was.

NORTHROP FRYE

Shakespeare's Romances: The Winter's Tale

The First Folio says it contains Shakespeare's comedies, histories, and tragedies, and that suggests a division of the main genres of Shakespeare's plays that has pretty well held the field ever since. The main change has been that we now tend to think of four very late plays, *Pericles*, *Cymbeline*, *The Winter's Tale* and *The Tempest*, as "romances," to distinguish them from the earlier comedies. These plays reflect a new vogue in playwriting, which Shakespeare probably established, and in which he was followed by younger writers, notably Fletcher and his collaborator Beaumont. One of these plays, Fletcher's *The Faithful Shepherdess*, has a preface that speaks of its being in a new form described as a "tragicomedy." These four romances have not always been favourites: only *The Tempest* has steadily held the stage, though it's often done so in some very curious distortions, and *Pericles* and *Cymbeline*, though superbly actable, are not very often performed even now.

Nevertheless, the romances are popular plays, not popular in the sense of giving the public what it wants, which is a pretty silly phrase anyway, but popular in the sense of coming down to the audience response at its most fundamental level. We noticed a primitive quality in *Measure for Measure* linking it with folk tales, and there's a close affinity between the romances and the most primitive (and therefore most enduring) forms of drama, like the puppet show. To mention some of their characteristics: first, there's a noticeable

From *Northrop Frye on Shakespeare*, edited by Robert Sandler, pp. 154–70. Copyright © 1986 by Northrop Frye.

3

scaling down of characters; that is, the titanic figures like Hamlet, Cleopatra, Falstaff and Lear have gone. Leontes and Posthumus are jealous, and very articulate about it, but their jealousy doesn't have the *size* that Othello's jealousy has: we're looking at people more on our level, saying and feeling the things we can imagine ourselves saying and feeling. Second, the stories are incredible: we're moving in worlds of magic and fairy tale, where anything can happen. Emotionally, they're as powerfully convincing as ever, but the convincing quality doesn't extend to the incidents. Third, there's a strong tendency to go back to some of the conventions of earlier plays, the kind that were produced in the 1580s: we noticed that *Measure for Measure* used one of these early plays as a source.

Fourth, the scaling down of characters brings these plays closer to the puppet shows I just mentioned. If you watch a good puppet show for very long you almost get to feeling that the puppets are convinced that they're producing all the sounds and movements themselves, even though you can see that they're not. In the romances, where the incidents aren't very believable anyway, the sense of puppet behaviour extends so widely that it seems natural to include a god or goddess as the string puller. Diana has something of this role in *Pericles*, and Jupiter has it in *Cymbeline*: *The Tempest* has a human puppeteer in Prospero. In *The Winter's Tale* the question "Who's pulling the strings?" is more difficult to answer, but it still seems to be relevant. The preface to that Fletcher play I mentioned says that in a "tragicomedy" introducing a god is "lawful," i.e., it's according to the "rules."

It may seem strange to think of Shakespeare rereading, as he clearly was, old plays that had gone out of fashion and been superseded by the highly sophisticated productions that came along in the early 1600s. But if we think of him as trying to recapture the primitive and popular basis of drama, it makes more sense. *Mucedorus* (anon.), for example, was a play written in the 1590s and revived (something rather unusual for that period) around 1610 or so, about the time of Shakespeare's romances. It tells the story of how a young prince fell in love with a picture of the heroine, a princess in a faraway country, and journeyed in disguise to her land to court her. It's advertised on its title page as "very delectable and full of mirth," as it has a clown who mixes his words.

The hero finds himself in the woods while the heroine and her suitor, a cowardly villain, are taking a walk. A bear appears; the heroine says whatever heroines say when they're confronted with bears; the cowardly villain mutters something like "Well, nice knowing you," and slopes off; there's a scuffle in the bushes and the hero appears carrying the bear's head. He says to the heroine, in effect: "Sorry this beast has been annoying you, but he won't be a problem now; by the way, here's his head, would you like it?" As far as we can make out from the dialogue and stage directions, the heroine says, "Thanks very much," and goes offstage lugging what one might think would be a somewhat messy object. As you see, it's all very delectable and full of mirth: it's a good-natured, harmless, simple-minded story, and the audience of Shakespeare's time ate it up. (So did readers: it went through seventeen Quartos.) But when we look at *The Winter's Tale* and see a stage direction like "Exit, pursued by a bear," we wonder if we're really in so very different a world, for all the contrast in complexity. Shakespeare himself didn't seem to think so: in the winding up of the two main stories in the play, he has a gentleman say of one, "This news which is called true is so like an old tale that the verity of it is in strong suspicion" (V.ii.27), and Paulina remarks of the other:

> That she is living,
> Were it but told you, should be hooted at
> like an old tale.
>   (V.iii.115–17)

I think the "romance" period of Shakespeare's production covers seven plays altogether. We know the approximate dates of Shakespeare's plays, but we can't pinpoint them all exactly in relation to the others: in any case a dramatist of his ability could have worked on more than one play at a time. The rest of this paragraph is guesswork, but not unreasonable guesswork. I think that after finishing *Antony and Cleopatra*, Shakespeare turned over the pages of Plutarch's *Lives* until his eye fell on the life of Coriolanus. Coriolanus makes a perfect contrast to Antony, because his tragedy is the tragedy of a genuine hero who rejects the theatrical, the continuous acting role that made Antony so magnetic a figure. Coriolanus performs amazing feats of valour, but he has to do everything himself: he can't hold an army together. There's an immature and mother-dominated streak in him that won't let him develop beyond the stage of a boy showing off. Plutarch's scheme, you remember, was to write "parallel" lives, taking two at a time, one Greek and the other Roman, who suggested resemblances or contrasts with each other, and then comparing them. The Greek counterpart of Coriolanus was Alcibiades, who was prominent in the Athens–Sparta war, and in the life of Alcibiades there's a digression telling the story of Timon the misanthrope or man hater.

Timon of Athens seems to me to be really Shakespeare's first romance: it differs completely from the great tragedies both in its choice of hero and, more important, in its structure. It breaks in two, like a diptych: we've seen that structure already in *Measure for Measure*. Timon is at the centre of his society, a wealthy man giving parties and being a patron of the arts, for the first half of the play; then he loses his money and his so-called friends drop quickly out of sight, and he's a hermit getting as far as he can from the human race for the second half. Of course we soon realize that he was completely isolated in his sociable phase, just as he's pestered with a great variety of visitors, cursing every one of them, in his hermit stage. The stylizing of the action is typical of the romances, and Timon himself, who dies offstage with a couple of lines of epitaph, is a scaled-down tragic hero.

Pericles is a curiously experimental play that recalls the early plays I mentioned, including an early play of Shakespeare's, *The Comedy of Errors*. *Pericles* is based, as the conclusion of the earlier comedy is, on the traditional story of Apollonius of Tyre. The poets who had retold this story included Gower, a contemporary of Chaucer, and Gower is brought on the stage to help tell the story of *Pericles*. This seems to be partly to suggest the authority of the story being told: you may not believe anything that happens in the story, but if someone gets up out of his grave after two hundred years to tell it to you, you don't start saying "yes, but." *Pericles* also tells its story partly by means of "dumb shows," like the one in the *Hamlet* mousetrap play. In *The Comedy of Errors* there's a priestess of Diana's temple in Ephesus, but no Diana: in *Pericles* Diana appears to the hero in a dream to tell him where to go next. I have no idea why the name Apollonius got changed to Pericles, except that Shakespeare probably made the change himself. The first two acts of *Pericles* don't sound at all like Shakespeare, but no collaborator has been suggested who wasn't considerably younger, and I'd expect the senior collaborator to be in charge of the general design of the play.

Cymbeline, like *Pericles*, is a "tragicomedy" (in fact it's included with the tragedies in the Folio). Cymbeline was king of Britain at the time of the birth of Christ, and, unlike Lear, is a fully historical character: his coins are in the British Museum. Nonetheless the main story told in the play is practically the story of Snow White. No dwarfs, but a very similar story, along with a jealousy story in which the villain, Iachimo, is, as perhaps his name suggests, a small-scale Iago.

The Winter's Tale and *The Tempest* we'll be dealing with next. *Henry VIII*, which seems to be later than *The Tempest*, is a history play assimilated to romance by concentrating on the central theme of the wheel of fortune, which keeps turning all through the play, and coming to an ironic conclusion with Anne Boleyn, Thomas Cromwell and Cranmer (two later beheaded and one burned alive) at the top of the wheel. There follows a very strange play called *The Two Noble Kinsmen*, a bitter, sardonic retelling of the story of Chaucer's *Knight's Tale*. We remember that the names Theseus and Hippolyta in *A Midsummer Night's Dream* were apparently taken from this tale, but nothing of its sombreness got into the earlier play. *The Two Noble Kinsmen* appeared, long after Shakespeare's death, in a Quarto saying it was the joint work of Shakespeare and Fletcher. Most scholars think that the play is mainly Fletcher's (it was included in the Beaumont and Fletcher Second Folio), but that the Quarto is right in assigning part of it to Shakespeare. After that the trail fades out, although there is a rumour of another collaboration with Fletcher which is lost. Many critics also think that *Henry VIII* is partly or largely Fletcher's, but I've never found this convincing, and I suspect that the motivation for believing it is partly that *The Tempest* seems a logical climax for the Shakespeare canon, and *Henry VIII* doesn't.

I spoke earlier of Greek New Comedy, which provided the original plots for Plautus and Terence. A spinoff from New Comedy was prose romance, which featured such themes as having someone of noble birth abandoned on a hillside as an infant, rescued and brought up as a shepherd, and eventually restored to his or her birthright, the essential documentary data having been thoughtfully placed beside the infant, and brought out when it's time for the story to end. Infants did get exposed on hillsides in ancient Greece, though it may not have happened as often, or with such hospitable shepherds, in life as it does in literature. One of these late Greek romances, by a writer named Heliodorus, was available to Shakespeare and his contemporaries in English, and is alluded to in *Twelfth Night*. The imitating of such romance formulas became fashionable in Elizabeth's time, and one such story was written by Robert Greene, Shakespeare's older contemporary, and called *Pandosto*. This story is the main source of *The Winter's Tale*, and its subtitle, *The Triumph of Time*, should also be kept in mind.

The first thing to notice about the play is that, like *Measure for Measure*, it breaks in the middle: there are two parts to the play, the first part all gloom and tragedy, the second part all romantic comedy. But in *Measure for Measure* there's no break in time: the action runs continuously through the same scene in the prison, where the deadlock between Claudio and Isabella is ended by the Duke's taking over the action. In *The Winter's Tale* Time himself is brought on the stage, at the beginning of the fourth act, to tell you that sixteen years have gone by, and that the infant you just saw exposed on the coast of Bohemia in a howling storm has grown up into a lovely young woman. It was still a general critical view that such breaks in the action of a play were absurd, and Shakespeare seems to be not just ignoring such views but deliberately flouting them.

The next thing to notice is that there are two breaks in the middle, and they don't quite coincide. (In speaking of breaks, of course, I don't mean that the play falls in two or lacks unity.) We do have the sixteen-year break at the end of the third act, but just before that there's another break, of a type much more like the one in *Measure for Measure*. We see Antigonus caught in a terrific storm and pursued by a bear: the linking of a bear with a tempest is an image in a speech of Lear's, and the storm here has something of the Lear storm about it, not just a storm but a world dissolving into chaos. After Antigonus's speech, the rhythm suddenly shifts from blank verse to prose, just as it does in *Measure for Measure*, and two shepherds come on the scene. So while we have the two parts of the time break, winter in Sicilia and spring in Bohemia sixteen years later, we also have another break suggesting that something is going on that's even bigger than that. We don't have a deputy dramatist like the Duke constructing the action of the second part. But we notice that Shakespeare follows his source in *Pandosto* quite closely up to the point corresponding to the two breaks, and after that he gets much more detached from it. Greene's Pandosto, the character corresponding to Leontes, never regenerates: toward the end he's attempting things like incest with his daughter, and his death is clearly a big relief all round.

Near the end of this play we have two scenes of the type critics call "recognition scenes," where some mystery at the beginning of the play is cleared up. One of these is the recognition of Perdita as a princess and daughter of Leontes. This recognition scene takes place offstage: it's not seen by us, but simply described in rather wooden prose by some "gentlemen," so however important to the plot it's clearly less important than the bigger recognition scene at the end, with Hermione and Leontes. Some of the things the gentlemen say, though, seem to be pointing to the real significance of the double break we've been talking about. One of them describes the emotional effect on all concerned of the discovery of the identity of Perdita, and says "they looked as they had heard of a world ransomed, or of one destroyed" (V.ii.14–15). Another, in recounting the death of Antigonus, says that the whole ship's crew was drowned: "so that all the instruments which aided to expose the child were even then lost when it was found" (i.e., by the shepherds) (V.ii.71–72). Tough on them, considering that they were only carrying out a king's orders, but, as we remember from the last speech of *Richard II*, kings have a lot of ways of keeping their hands clean. We notice that back in the scene where the shepherds find the baby, the shepherd who does find it says to the one who saw the bear eating Antigonus, "thou mettest with things dying, I with things newborn" (III.iii.112). The New Arden editor says that this is just a simple statement of fact, whatever a "fact" may be in a play like this. The two halves of the play seem to be not just Sicilian winter and Bohemian spring, but a death-world and a life-world.

Ben Jonson remarked to his friend Drummond, as an example of Shakespeare's carelessness in detail, that in this play he'd given a seacoast to Bohemia, which was a landlocked country. It's just possible that Shakespeare knew this too: in *The Tempest* he also gives a seacoast to the inland Duchy of Milan. *The Winter's Tale* was one of many plays performed in connection with the festivities attending the marriage of King James's daughter, Elizabeth, to a prince who came from that part of the world. In a few years the Thirty Years' War broke out and he lost his kingdom, and was known thereafter as "the winter king of Bohemia." (However, that story has a long-term happy ending: it was through this marriage that the House of Hanover came to the British throne a century later.) The names Sicilia and Bohemia came from *Pandosto*, but Shakespeare reverses their relation to the characters. I doubt that the name Bohemia means much of anything, and the setting of the play doesn't stay there: it changes back to Sicilia for the end of the play, so that we begin with Sicilia dying and end with Sicilia newborn. And I think the name Sicilia may mean something. It was in Sicily that the literary pastoral—and this play is full of pastoral imagery—originated, and it was in Sicily that the beautiful maiden Proserpine was kidnapped and carried off to the lower world by Pluto, forcing her mother, Ceres, to search all over the upper world for her. In this play Hermione doesn't search, but she doesn't come to life either (or whatever she does) until Perdita, whose name means the lost maiden, is said to be found.

We start off, both in the prose introductory scene and the dialogue of the main scene that follows it, with a heavy, cloying, suet-pudding atmosphere that feels like a humid day before a thunderstorm. Leontes, king of Sicilia, is entertaining Polixenes, king of Bohemia, as a guest, and they're crawling over each other with demonstrations of affection. Leontes' queen, Hermione, is just about to give birth, and Polixenes has been visiting for nine months, so it's technically possible for Leontes to do some perverted mental arithmetic. Before long, with no warning, the storm strikes, and Leontes, who's been playing the gracious host role up to now, suddenly turns insanely jealous, setting in motion an extremely grim train of events. In a romance, we just accept Leontes' jealousy as we would a second subject in a piece of music: it's there, and that's all there is to it, except to keep on listening. There are references to a period of innocence in the childhood of the two kings, then some teasing about the role of their two wives in losing their innocence, and finally Hermione says to Polixenes:

> Th' offences we have made you do, we'll answer,
> If you first sinn'd with us, and that with us
> You did continue fault, and that you slipp'd not
> With any but with us.
> (I.ii.83–86)

In its context, all this is harmless badinage, but to a poisoned mind every syllable suggests a horrible leering innuendo, as well as an in-joke that Leontes is excluded from.

Leontes is caught in the strong tricks of imagination that Theseus spoke of in *A Midsummer Night's Dream*, where nothing, under the pressure of what Leontes calls "affection" or emotional stress, consolidates into something, and creates an irrational fantasy. The wife of Greene's Pandosto does at least hang around her guest's bedchamber, but Leontes has nothing in the way of "evidence" of that kind, and even the most perverse director couldn't give us a justified Leontes trapped by designing women. We notice how this creation of something out of nothing is associated with the contact senses: he says he smells and feels and tastes his situation, but seeing and hearing, the primary senses of the objective, he takes less account of.

Here again we start rolling down a steep slide, as in *King Lear*, except that in *King Lear* the degenerating is in the king's outer circumstances, whereas here it's in his character. Before long Leontes is trying to get his courtier Camillo to murder Polixenes; foiled by Camillo's flight, he turns coward and (as he says explicitly) is resolved to take it out on Hermione. He hits perhaps his lowest point when he complains that he can't sleep, and wonders if having Hermione burnt alive would give him rest. Later he speaks of burning the infant Perdita, who's just been born in the middle of this hullabaloo, and when Hermione's friend Paulina speaks her mind, he threatens to burn her too. Other images of useless sacrifice run all through this part of the play. Leontes is also obsessed by the notion that people are laughing at him behind his back (which of course they are, though not for the reason he thinks). He can say, however, "How blest am I" in acquiring his totally illusory knowledge of good and evil.

And yet every so often the fog clears a bit, and we realize that the Paulina-Leontes relation is really that of a nanny and a child in a screaming tantrum. Leontes says to Paulina's husband, Antigonus:

I charg'd thee that she should not come about me.
I knew she would.
   (II.iii.43–44)

There is a quite funny scene where Paulina sweeps in, Leontes orders her out, a swarm of male courtiers make futile efforts at pushing her, and Paulina brushes them off like insects while Leontes blusters. We realize that as soon as he gets rid of his obsession he'll be quite a decent person again, though one doesn't go through such things unmarked. At least he has had the sense to consult the oracle of Apollo, which tells him the exact truth about his situation. But Leontes has fallen into what he calls, in the last lines of the play, a "gap in time," and so the timing goes all wrong.

First comes the news of Mamillius's death from shame at the accusation of his mother. He seems a trifle young for such a reaction, but this is romance.

It's this news that shatters Leontes' ugly world: nothing has lessened his affection for this boy, and he has never seriously questioned his legitimacy. Now he's in a very bad situation for a king, without an heir to succeed him. For very soon afterward comes the news of Hermione's death, brought by Paulina. "She's dead, I'll swear't," says Paulina—a remark we might put away for future reference. Then again, the machinery has already been set in motion to make Antigonus go to Bohemia to leave the infant Perdita on Polixenes' territorial doorstep. We notice that Hermione returns to visit Antigonus as a ghost in a dream—by Jacobean dramatic conventions a pretty reliable sign that she's really dead. As Antigonus has not heard the oracle's report, he disappears into a bear, thinking that Polixenes after all must be the infant's father.

The Winter's Tale is set in a pagan and Classical world, where Apollo's oracle is infallibly inspired, and where the man who survived the flood is referred to by his Ovidian name of Deucalion and not his Biblical name of Noah. As always, Shakespeare is not rigorously consistent: there are Biblical allusions, such as Perdita's to the Gospel passage about the sun shining on all alike, which may be considered unconscious, but Polixenes' reference to Judas Iscariot hardly could be. We also seem to be back to "anointed kings," and the awfulness of injuring them: doubtless the more Shakespeare's reputation grew, the more carefully he had to look out for long ears in the audience. But no one can miss the pervading imagery or the number of links with Ovid's *Metamorphoses*: in this play we're not only in the atmosphere of folk tale, as we were in *Measure for Measure*, but in that of Classical mythology as well.

At the centre of the play there's the common folk-tale theme of the calumniated mother. This is a cut-down version of a myth in which a hero or heroine has a divine father and a human mother, so that the man who would normally expect to be the father becomes jealous and wants to kill at least the child, if not the mother too. So the calumniated-mother theme is usually connected with a threatened-birth theme, which is also in the play. We're reminded of two famous Ovidian myths in particular. One is the myth of Ceres and Proserpine, already mentioned, and referred to by Perdita in speaking of her spring flowers. (I give the Ovidian Latin names: the Greek ones, Demeter and Persephone or Kore, may be more familiar now.) The other is the story of Pygmalion and the statue Venus brings to life for him. There is another faint mythical theme in the resemblance between Florizel and Mamillius, a resemblance commented on by Leontes. After Leontes has lost his own son and heir, Florizel becomes his heir in the old-fashioned mythical way, by coming from afar, marrying the king's daughter, and succeeding by what is called mother right.

There are two main stories in the play, contrapuntally linked as usual. One is a straight New Comedy story of Perdita and her lover, Florizel; of how their marriage is blocked by parental opposition, and released by the discovery that Perdita is really a princess after all. The other is the story of the separation and reunion of Leontes and Hermione, which, again as usual in Shakespeare, seems to be the more important story of the two. The cultural environment is more extra-Christian than pre-Christian as in *King Lear*. A tragedy reveals the impotence of the Classical gods; a comedy can give us something of the sunnier side of paganism. The opening dialogue refers to the boyhood of Leontes and Polixenes as a state of innocence that was clear even of original sin.

In *King Lear* we met two levels of nature: an upper level of human nature, which includes many things that in Shakespeare's day would also be called "art," but which are natural to man, and a lower level associated with predatory animals and what we call the law of the jungle. In *The Winter's Tale* there are also two aspects of nature, but they're in more of a parallel than a hierarchical relation. Philosophers have always distinguished two categories of nature. One is nature as a structure or system, the physical aspect of it; the other is the biological aspect, nature as the total power of growth, death and renewed life. They're sometimes called *natura naturata* and *natura naturans*. In *King Lear*, again, the upper, human level is associated with nature as an order; the lower level is associated mainly with ferocity, Tennyson's nature "red in tooth and claw." But in *The Winter's Tale* we have the story of Florizel and Perdita associated with a genial nature of renewing power, the other aspect being more emphasized in the Leontes-Hermione one. There are still different levels, but these exist in both the forms of nature emphasized in the two stories.

There seem to be three main levels in all. In the Leontes-Hermione world, there is a low or demonic level in the chaos released by Leontes' jealousy, a world full of treachery and murder, pointless sacrifice, sterility and utterly needless pain. This is a world of fantasy below reason, the imagination working in its diseased or "imaginary" aspect. Above this is a middle world of rationality, where the court is functioning normally. This middle world is represented particularly by two characters, Camillo and Paulina, who, like Kent in *King Lear*, combine outspoken honest criticism with a fierce loyalty. Above that again is the world we enter in the final scene, a world of imagination in its genuine creative sense, as far above reason as jealousy is below it.

In the Florizel-Perdita world, which is set mainly in Bohemia, there are also three main levels of the action. At the bottom is Autolycus the thief, by no means as sinister a figure as the jealous Leontes, but still something of a nuisance. He would like to be the standard New Comedy tricky servant, but, as I remarked earlier, Shakespeare doesn't care much for this character type, and manoeuvres the main action around him. He lives in a somewhat mindless present: for the life to come, he says, he sleeps out the thought of it.

Above him comes the normally functioning level of this world, which is represented primarily by the sheep-shearing festival (IV.iv). The imagery of this scene is that of the continuous fertilizing power of nature, with Perdita distributing flowers appropriate to all ages, and with a dance of twelve "satyrs" at the end, who perhaps celebrate the entire twelve-month year. Perdita seems, her lover tells her, like the goddess Flora presiding over "a meeting of the petty gods." In her turn Perdita speaks with the most charming frankness of wanting to strew her lover with flowers, not "like a corse," but as "a bank for love to lie and play on." She has Autolycus warned not to use any "scurrilous words" in his tunes, and while of course the primary meaning is that she is a fastidious girl who dislikes obscenity, her motives are magical as well as moral: a festive occasion should not be spoiled by words of ill omen. The top level of this world, the recognition and marriage, we do not see, but merely hear it reported, as mentioned earlier.

In the Florizel-Perdita world the relation of art to nature has a different aspect at each of these levels. When Autolycus first enters (IV.iii) he is singing the superb "When daffodils begin to peer" song, one of the finest of all spring songs, and we welcome this harbinger of spring as we do the cuckoo, who is also a thief. Later he comes in with a peddler's pack of rubbish, which he calls "trumpery." We should note this word, because it's used again in a similar context by Prospero in *The Tempest*: it's connected with *tromper*, deceive, and, at the risk of sounding moralizing, we can say that his ribbons and such are "artificial" in the modern derogatory sense of an art that is mainly a corruption of nature. He also produces a number of broadside ballads, which were quite a feature of Elizabethan life: they were the tabloid newspapers of the time, and some of the alleged news they carried was so extravagant that Shakespeare's examples are hardly caricatures. It is on the next level that Polixenes offers his Renaissance idealistic view of the relation of art to nature: in grafting, we use art in implanting a bud on a stock, but the power of nature is what makes it grow. The emphasis on the power of nature is appropriate, even though Perdita will have nothing to do with any interference from art on "great creating nature." And in the reported recognition, the gentlemen tell us that such wonderful things have happened "that ballad-makers cannot be able to express it." So it seems that Autolycus and his preposterous ballads have something to do with the function of art in this world after all.

In the Leontes-Hermione story we have at the bottom the parody art of Leontes' jealousy making something out of nothing, a demonic reversal of the divine creation. On the middle level we have, in the conversation of the gentlemen, a very curious reference to a painted statue of Hermione made by Julio Romano. Romano was an actual painter, widely touted as the successor of Raphael, but the reason for mentioning his name here eludes us: perhaps

there was some topical reason we don't know about. He is said to be a fanati-
cally realistic worker in the technique we'd now call *trompe l'oeil*: there's the
word *tromper* again. If what we're told is what we're to believe, there's no
statue at all, so there was no point in mentioning him, although the conception of art as an illusion of nature perhaps fits this level and aspect of the
story. The final scene involves all the arts, in the most striking contrast to the
Perdita-Florizel recognition: the action takes place in Paulina's chapel; we are
presented with what we're told is painting and sculpture; music and oracular
language are used at appropriate moments; and another contemporary meaning of the word "art," magic, so important in *The Tempest*, is also referred to.

If we look at the words that get repeated, it seems as though the word
"wonder" has a special connection with the Florizel-Perdita story, and the
word "grace" with the Leontes-Hermione one. "Grace" has a bewildering
variety of meanings in Shakespearean English, many of them obsolete. In
the opening dialogue Hermione uses it so frequently and pointedly that we
don't just hear it: it seems to stand out from its context. When she becomes
the victim of Leontes' fantasy, she says that what's happening to her is for her
"better grace," and when she finally speaks at the end of the play, what she
says is a prayer for the graces of the gods to descend. We may, perhaps, isolate
from all the possible meanings two major ones: first, the power of God (the
Classical gods in this play) that makes the redemption of humanity possible,
and, second, the quality that distinguishes civilized life, of the kind "natural"
to man, from the untutored or boorish.

Let's see what we have now:

A. The Leontes-Hermione story of the order of nature; winter
tale of "grace."

B. The Florizel-Perdita story of the power and fertility of nature;
spring tale of "wonder."

Upper Level
A. Transformation of Hermione from illusion to reality; union of
all the arts.

B. Recognition of Perdita as princess by birth (i.e., nature); ballads
of wonder.

Middle Level
A. Court world of Camillo and Paulina; art as Romano's illusion
of nature.

B. World of festival; image of art as grafting or attachment to power of nature.

Lower Level
A. Illusory world of Leontes' jealousy: parody of imaginative creation. Mamillius's aborted "winter's tale."

B. Autolycus: pure present; songs of spring; also "trumpery" or arts corrupting nature.

In the final scene, what we are apparently being told is that Paulina has kept Hermione hidden for sixteen years, Hermione consenting to this because the oracle seemed to hint that Perdita would survive. There was never any statue. But other things seem to be going on that don't quite fit that story. In the first place, Paulina's role, partly actor-manager and partly priestess, seems grotesquely ritualistic and full of pretentious rhetoric on that assumption; some of the things she says are really incantations:

> Music, awake her; strike!
> 'Tis time; descend; be stone no more; approach. . . .
> (V.iii.98–99)

Later she remarks that Hermione is not yet speaking, and then pronounces the words "Our Perdita is found," as though they were the charm that enabled her to speak. In several comedies of Shakespeare, including this one and *The Tempest*, the action gets so hard to believe that a central character summons the rest of the cast into—I suppose—the green room afterward, where, it is promised, all the difficulties will be cleared away. The audience can just go home scratching their heads. Here it looks as though the green room session will be quite prolonged; Leontes says:

> But how, is to be question'd; for I saw her,
> As I thought, dead; and have in vain said many
> A prayer upon her grave.
> (V.iii.139–41)

One might perhaps visualize Leontes saying, "Do you mean to tell me," etc., then erupting into fury at the thought of all those wasted prayers and starting the whole action over again.

We notice the importance of the word "faith" in this play: it's applied by Camillo to Leontes' fantasy, which is below reason, and by Florizel to his fidelity to Perdita despite parental opposition, which, he says explicitly, is a "fancy" above reason. And in this final scene Paulina tells her group that they must awaken their faith, which would hardly make sense unless Hermione were actually coming to life. Such things don't happen in real life, but they happen in myths, and *The Winter's Tale* is a mythical play. We seem to be getting two versions of the scene at once: which is real and which is the illusion? On the stage there's no difference: the illusion and the reality are the same thing. But if even Leontes can say "how, is to be questioned," what price us as we leave the theatre?

I've spoken of the popularity of Ovid's *Metamorphoses* as a kind of poet's bible, and in no play of Shakespeare, except perhaps *A Midsummer Night's Dream*, is its influence more obvious and insistent than it is here. This is partly because poetic language, a language of myth and metaphor, is the language best adapted to a world of process and change, where everything keeps turning into something else. Even in *King Lear* we saw that a new kind of language was getting born out of all that suffering and horror. Here something equally mysterious is going on, but in the context of comedy. To use Theseus's words "apprehend" and "comprehend": in this final scene we "apprehend" that we're looking at a real Hermione, and "comprehend" that she's been hidden by Paulina for sixteen years and there's no statue. That's the "credible" version: we call it credible because there's nothing to believe. Or, perhaps, we "apprehend" that first there was Hermione, then there was a statue of her after she died, and now there's Hermione again. How do we "comprehend" that? Obviously not by trying to "believe" it.

In Ovid most of the "metamorphoses" are changes downward, from some kind of personal or human being into a natural object, a tree, a bird or a star. But there can also be metamorphosis upward. This happens every year when winter turns into spring and new forms of life appear: this kind of metamorphosis we've been associating with the story of Perdita. The story of Hermione seems to imply something more: new possibilities of expanded vision that such people as Shakespeare have come into the world to suggest to us.

As so often in Shakespeare, expanded vision seems to have a good deal to do with time and the ways we experience it. We noted that *The Triumph of Time* was the subtitle of Greene's *Pandosto*, and the early part of the play stresses such words as "push" and "wild" (meaning rash), which suggest a continuous violation of the normal rhythms of time. Then Time appears as chorus: perhaps it is he, not Apollo, who controls the action. We might even give the two parts of the play the Proustian subtitles of *Time Lost* and *Time Regained*. The concluding speech, by Leontes, speaks of the "gap of time" he fell into with his jealousy, and ends "Hastily lead away." There is no time to be lost, once one has found it again.

RUTH NEVO

Cymbeline: *The Rescue of the King*

All creatures born of our fantasy, in the last analysis, are nothing but ourselves.

(Schiller)

There is a "plethora of story-lines," as Barbara Mowatt puts it, in *Cymbeline*:

> The Snow White tale of a princess, her evil stepmother, a home in the woods and a deathlike sleep; a Romeo-and-Juliet–like tragedy of a banished lover, an unwanted suitor, deaths and near-deaths; a medieval folktale of a chastity-wager and an evil Italian villain. (1976, 55)

There are also Roman legions and (real) British chronicle history. The components of these stories are quite regular features of romance narrative, but in *Cymbeline* they generate weirdly replicative configurations: Imogen and Posthumus both survive two lost brothers, both are orphans, and both have been brought up in the same household by a step- or foster parent, as have one set, Imogen's, of lost brothers. We make the acquaintance of a foster father, a bereaved father, a blocking father, a substitute father-mother (Belarius), a surrogate father (Lucius), a father-god, a visionary father-and-mother who

From *Shakespeare's Other Language*, pp. 62–94, 157–58. Copyright © 1987 by Ruth Nevo.

17

appear to Posthumus in a dream or hallucination, and a mother-father in the shape of the King who at the end announces himself, in wonder "A mother to the birth of three" (V.v.369). A poison disguised as a prophylactic becomes a cordial whose effects appear lethal; into (or out of) the play's orbit floats a trunkless head, a headless trunk, and a false trunk from which a man emerges; Imogen is the victim, twice, of a species of (unconsummated) bed-trick, once with a slanderer sent by her husband to test her, and once with the dead body of her rejected suitor whom she takes to be her husband; she is wakened by an aubade (though she has not been in bed with a lover) and laid to rest with an elegy (though she is not dead); Posthumus changes from Roman to British clothing and back a number of times; and there are more recognitions and revelations in Act V than most readers can confidently count. Would one not be justified in regarding repetition of such high frequency as a kind of representational stutter? Or does the play precisely thus speak of what it can only partly say?

Cymbeline presents some of the knottiest problems in Shakespeare genre criticism, appearing to be neither fish, flesh nor good red herring; readable neither as history, comedy nor romance. Though placed after *Pericles* in the accepted chronology of the final plays, it is in many ways more akin to the earlier *All's Well* than to the other three romances. As in *All's Well*, the heroine sets out in pursuit of an errant husband and the hub of the interest lies in the affairs of the young married couple, who are estranged. Yet much is made of the return of Cymbeline's long-lost sons and the family reunions, as in the romances, which bridge the wide gap of time inserted into the dramatic action by the interwoven desires of two generations. As in *All's Well* it is important that a wasteland-sick king is made well. *Cymbeline* is the last of the plays to make a bold young woman, rather than her father, its main protagonist. In that respect Imogen is more akin to the independent daughters of the earlier courtship comedies than to the thaumaturgic daughters of the three last plays; yet she is far from being free of a controlling parent as are Beatrice, Viola, Olivia and Rosalind. She is what one might call a post-tragic heroine, abused, vilified, hunted, and not in possession of crucial knowledge. She may know what she is doing when she defies her tyrant father ("I beseech you, sir, / Harm not yourself with your vexation, / I am senseless of your wrath" (1.1.133–5)), but she (like everyone else in *Cymbeline*, indeed)[1] is at every point unaware of or deceived about the major facts effecting her situation. Where Rosalind and Viola act out their maverick fantasies with a blithe insouciance, adopting their boy's garb as a ploy to be enjoyed, while it lasts, for the mastery it gives them, Imogen is driven by desperate straits into hers. She wears, as we shall see, her cap and hose with a difference. It is a difference, I shall argue, which requires for its understanding a radical departure in critical method.

According to Johnson's magisterial opinion:

> This play has many just sentiments, some natural dialogues, and
> some pleasing scenes, but they are obtained at the expense of much
> incongruity. To remark the folly of the fiction, the absurdity of
> the conduct, the confusion of the names and manners of different
> times, and the impossibility of the events in any system of life,
> were to waste criticism upon unresisting imbecility, upon faults too
> evident for detection, and too gross for aggravation. ((1756) 1958,
> 8, 908)

Traditional criticism has not found it easy to circumvent Johnson's rugged
rationalism, has indeed very often negotiated itself into culs-de-sac in the
attempt. Nosworthy, for instance, pointing out that Johnson failed to take
into account the romance genre of the play, in terms of which Johnson's
defects are "among the prime virtues" ((1955) 1980, xlviii) finds himself
lauding the "symbolic" or schematic characters (the Queen, Cloten, Belarius
and the boys, Cymbeline himself) as "the achievement" of Shakespeare's
object, namely, "to create characters flattened, insulated, idealized, and
unreal, who belong to no normal system of life, but to a world of romance"
(lvi), while in consequence the greater realism of Posthumus, Imogen and
Iachimo is found to be out of place. Valiantly fighting a rearguard action
over the awkward three, Nosworthy dismisses Iachimo as no more than "a
stock figure" (lvii), finds Posthumus "one of the dullest of Shakespeare's
heroes," who "never really comes to life" (lix), and Imogen, who "defeated
Shakespeare's intentions by coming to life," "sadly out of character in this
play." She is, he says, "enchanting in her cumulative effect," though "a various and erratic tissue of inconsistencies" upon analysis (lxi). It is no wonder
then, that criticism thus wound in its own toils "has sometimes had to own
itself confounded when it has asked why Shakespeare fashioned the play as
he did, or even why he fashioned it at all" (xi). The answer is found in the
appeal to a transcendent anagogue which will absolve the play of the defects
just attributed to it. Thus *Cymbeline* is not to be regarded (as is customary)
"as an oddly unaccountable lapse" in the Shakespearean *oeuvre* but as one
of "his supreme utterances" (lxxviii) and this for the reason that it is "purely
Shakespearean in its recognition that life itself is not a coherent pattern. . .
but a confused series of experiences, good and evil, grave and gay, momen-
tous and trivial," whose end is a "vision of perfect tranquillity, a partial com-
prehension of that Peace which passeth all understanding" (lxxix, lxxxiii).

Such a shift of ground is familiar in the criticism of the romances as
an alternative to hard-nosed Johnson. Barbara Mowatt urges us to renounce

our expectations of rationality and probability, of "syllogism" when we come to the late dramas of Shakespeare, so that we may experience "life in its full complexity—tragic and comic, wonderful and terrible, real and unreal, and as unfathomable as Bottom's dream" (1976, 119). Reginald Foakes invokes "the mysterious operation of a providence not understood by the characters" as the only way to explain "the inconsistencies, contradictions and coincidences of the action," its "dream-like strangeness" and unexpectedness, so that in the end we have "an overall consistent and intelligible dramatic mode" which, "as a whole, is like the action of our own lives" (1971, 117–18).

These positions are really criticism with its back to the wall; certainly with its syllogistic back to the wall. A play is (or should be) logical and life-like. *Cymbeline* is not logical and lifelike. Therefore it is a special kind of play which is like life. Interestingly enough, both of the critics just quoted speak of dream, of dreamlike features, yet they employ interpretative procedures solely appropriate to discourse rationally ordered, mimetically feasible and obedient to the logic of noncontradiction, of time, place, causality and condition. Suppose we attempt to adapt a hermeneutic of dream analysis, or a model of psychoanalytic discourse for the construing of the "strangenesses," absurdities, coincidences, improbabilities in this play? Suppose we assume that dramatis personae, like personae in dreams may be composite or split figures, doubles or proxies for each other, and that language ambiguous, or evocatively charged or polysemous or conspicuously figured may indeed mean more, or other than it ostensibly says?[2]

Certainly *Cymbeline* is an excellent text with which to test such hypotheses. We will go far to find a better. It is my project in the following pages to argue that the strange, the outlandish, the incredibly coincidental, the absurd, grotesque or uncanny can be read, not as excrescences to be somehow explained away, but as profoundly meaningful. To ape for a moment the structuralist type of terminology, and to launch a companion to rhemes, semes and phonemes, such oddities could perhaps be regarded as "dremes" emerging into the ordinary carriage of the plot and the ordinary behaviour of its agents with their own ulterior and covert messages. It is not important, nor is it possible to determine to what extent the author was conscious of them. It is for the purpose of being able to talk about such messages, without determining their status, that we require the notion of a textual unconscious. It is just because *Cymbeline* is replete with representational anomalies, discords and dissonances, presents us with a medley of melodies and chords diverging and converging in a bewildering polyphony, that it can provide a test case for the value of the concept. The question is can we unbind this text, feel our way toward a unifying, organizing fantasy which we can deduce as having generated the play and which, made conscious, is capable of reanimating in us a corresponding working through process? A hundred years of psychoanalysis have accumulated a vast archive of instances analogous to the adventures of our protagonists, and provided a lexicon, but it will not be a matter of deciphering a code or of diagnosing a neurosis in a dramatic character. It is rather a matter of feeling our way into a state of mind, or states of mind, in which the oddities and discrepancies suddenly "figure"; it is a matter, to add a significant letter to Lacan's dictum, of discovering "the 'unsaid' that lies in the (w)holes of the discourse" (1977, 93).

In the first instance this entails psychological analysis, at whatever level, of the motivations and dispositions of the play's protagonists. "What does Imogen (or Posthumus, or Cymbeline) want?" is a primary question, but we at once become aware that it is less important to inquire what, for instance, Iachimo or Cloten or Belarius want, than to figure out what they represent within the imagined worlds of the protagonists. Just as dreams are always about the dreamer, so there is always a central ego for a play to be about. It was precisely the reversal of this hierarchy which was witty and intriguing in Tom Stoppard's *Rosencrantz and Guildenstern are Dead*.

Our first oddity, then, is the play's eponym. Why is the drama named for King Cymbeline, when it is not in any strict sense a history play conventionally named after a reigning monarch, and when he himself, save for his initial banishment of Posthumus, is a passive figure, browbeaten and henpecked by his wicked Queen and incomparably less prominent in the play's action than his sorely tried daughter? About her importance there will no doubt be little argument. The Imogenolatry of nineteenth-century Shakespeare criticism,[3] its roots in defensive Victorian (and Renaissance) idealization to which we no longer subscribe, is still pervasive in the criticism as witness to her centrality, however we may wish to account for it. Yet the King is the pivot and cynosure of all the revelations and recognitions in Act V, suddenly a rival epicentre. The virtual absence of His Majesty the King in the play which is named for him is thus a signifier which demands attention. I believe that the central ego in *Cymbeline* is, ultimately, Cymbeline, but that, for reasons which will presently appear, that ego is in abeyance, in temporary suspension, as it were, behind the three plots through which *Cymbeline* unfolds.

The three plots in *Cymbeline*: the individual marital (Imogen and Posthumus); the familial (the kidnapped brothers); and the national (the rebellion of a province against the Empire) are interlocked with a craft which it is customary to admire; but it is worth noticing that they do not conduct themselves in the least in the way Shakespearean subplots usually do. We are accustomed to three- or even four-tier mirroring structures, as in *A Midsummer Night's Dream*, or *As You Like It*, or *Henry IV*, where goings-on at the socially lower, or more "foolish" levels counterpoint or comment

upon the doings, and sayings at the upper level.[4] In *Cymbeline* there is no
such ramification or hierarchy. Rather there seem to be issues which find
expression over and over again, and so suggest the existence of an obsessive
need, a compulsion. The play is like a jigsaw puzzle whose broken-apart and
mixed-up pieces must be matched and put together. It is like its families.
Children are orphaned, or kidnapped, parents bereaved, a wife and husband
separated, siblings parted. The confederation of an empire and its province
disrupted. Fragmentation is brought to a phantasmagoric extreme; even
bodies are dismembered and not recognized. It is worth noticing that the
word "thing" as an epithet applied to persons—"Thou basest thing" (I.i.125),
"O disloyal thing" (131), "This imperceiverant thing" (IV.i.14), "Slight thing
of Italy" (V.iv.64), for instance, occurs in *Cymbeline* more often than in any
other of Shakespeare's plays. Notice, in contradistinction to this reification,
Posthumus' culminating organic image when he finds himself and Imogen:
"Hang there like fruit, my soul," (V.v.263). The personae, disassociated parts
of dismembered families, do not recognize each other, or themselves, are
confused about their roles, their "parts," especially Posthumus and Imogen.
Or else they are partial persons, clearly projective. The Queen is a poison
mother, a projection of infantile fantasy. The King is a *nom du père*, a *non du
père*, to borrow Lacan's extraordinarily apt witticism, but in his absence other
father figures keep springing up. The recognition scenes at the end, until
the very last, are partial, piecemeal, kaleidoscopic; people are, and are not,
recognized. The King finds Lucius' page, his daughter, hauntingly familiar.
Posthumus sees, though he does not recognize, in the feminine beauty of
Belarius' sons the resemblance to their sister, his wife. The family, Meredith
Skura notes, "is so important that characters cannot even imagine themselves without one" (1980, 205). Their problem, however, is how to imagine
themselves within one. Hence, in the course of the drama, families keep
being reconstituted, partly, or by proxy, in caves, in visions, in disguise.

Let us pursue the fortunes of the initially presented protagonists. We
shall not reach the deepest level of fantasy until we have worked through the
more manifest meanings and motivations which lead us to what they screen.
But it is to the young lovers that the play first solicits our attention.

The story of Posthumus Leonatus, a fatherless youth whose very name
orphans him, is the *Bildungsroman* of a young man whose manhood is under
inspection. He is of noble lineage but cannot, as yet, be "delve[d] to the root"
(1.1.28). He is put to the test first of all by the banishment which immediately follows his marriage. Skura is wrong when she says that Posthumus' first
mistake is to "usurp his proper place" (in his foster family) "when he elopes
with Imogen" (1980, 209). He precisely does not elope with her. He allows
himself to be separated from her and leaves her in virtual imprisonment in

Britain. The Gentleman who lavishes praise upon him, expressing, he says, the general view, announces that he is a creature such

> As, to seek through the regions of the earth
> For one his like, there would be something failing
> In him that should compare (I.i.20–2)

The syntax is disorientingly ambiguous. Anyone like him would, by virtue of the likeness, possess a failing? Anyone assuming to be compared with him would, by virtue of the comparison, be found wanting? We settle, of course for the second, but we cannot quite rid our minds of the other possibility the syntax and lineation allows. This is followed by a very curious phrase in the Gentleman's assurance to his interlocutor that he is not exaggerating:

> I do extend him, sir, within himself,
> Crush him together rather than unfold
> His measure duly. (25–7)

This suggests some malleable object rather than the admired scion of a noble stock; and we learn, in Pisanio's account of Cloten's attack upon him, that "My master rather play'd than fought / And had no help of anger" (I.i.161–3). What are we being told, in so devious a manner, about Posthumus the universally praised? Some doubts about the "eagle" quality of Imogen's lover must surely enter one's mind, the more especially since her own defiance of her father has been outspoken and unequivocal. Interestingly enough, his own first words to his beloved betray a self-consciousness about the very question of manliness:

> My queen, my mistress!
> O lady, weep no more, lest I give cause
> To be suspected of more tenderness
> Than doth become a man. (I.i.92–5)

These two newly-wed quasi-siblings, violently separated, their marriage unconsummated, mark their parting with the gift of significantly symbolic transitional objects. She gives him a diamond, her mother's, to be parted with only after her death, when he will woo her successor; he, invoking death rather than such a possibility, "imprisons" her arm with a bracelet, a "manacle of love" (122). He needs to "possess" her (his preoccupation with possessions is evident throughout), and is uncertain of his tenure. She needs to foster and cherish him, but, as we touchingly learn when she relives, with Pisanio, the

distancing of his ship, worrying about getting letters, reimagining his diminishing image, envying the handkerchief he kissed and waved, mourning the
lost opportunity to bask in a lover's appreciation, she needs him as a mirror in
which she can see herself, recognize herself as cherished and valued.

> I did not take my leave of him, but had
> Most pretty things to say. Ere I could tell him
> How I would think on him at certain hours. . . .
>   or I could make him swear
> The shes of Italy should not betray
> Mine interest and his honor. . . .
>   or ere I could
> Give him that parting kiss which I had set
> Betwixt two charming words, comes in my father,
> And like the tyrannous breathing of the north
> Shakes all our buds from growing. (I.iii.25–37, passim)

They are buds in their youthfulness, in their youthful narcissism, and
they are "shaken" from growing by the blocking father that Cymbeline is to
them. Buds that are kept from growing together, grow apart, revealing fatal
dissonances in their relationship, and disequilibrium in their personalities.

That Posthumus allowed himself to be torn from his bride, did not
snatch her to him and take flight with her, is, of course, a donnée of the
play; but much, and with a certain emphasis, is made of it. In Act II, scene
iv Philario asks Posthumus what means he is taking to overcome the King's
interdict. "Not any," is the reply,

> but abide the change of time,
> Quake in the present winter's state, and wish
> That warmer days would come. (4–6)

This is followed by an oxymoron which reads suspiciously like a slip of
the tongue. "In these fear'd hopes," says Posthumus, "I barely gratify your
love" (6–7). Which emotion, if any, is dominant? fear, hope, doubt? If it is
felt that pessimism or trepidation is sufficiently accounted for by a state of
fatherlessness, propertylessness and banishment, it is worth recalling that
Imogen refers to him "when he was here" as "inclin[ing] to sadness, and
oft-times / Not knowing why" (I.vi.61–3) and that the sigh that escapes her:
"O, that husband!/My supreme crown of grief . . . . Had I been thief-stol'n,
/ As my two brothers, happy!" (3–6), makes her cause of grief anaphorically
her husband himself rather than, or at least as well as, his absence; and while

it ostensibly refers to the stealing away of her brothers in the past, contains the suggestion of a wished-for stealing away of herself in the present. Posthumus, who speaks very highly of his countrymen as formidable warriors, lacks himself, it seems, sufficient pugnacity to shine as a lover, and it is as a chivalric lover that he is put to the test in Rome by the challenge of a mischief-making Italian.

There is much to be learned from the provocation scene. First of all it is not, evidently, the first such occasion, but a repetition of a similar chivalric affirmation of the superlative virtue of a lady, which would have ended at sword's point save for the intervention of the Frenchman. Iachimo, subtle manipulator, who has already disparaged Posthumus before his entrance, sets his trap cunningly. The target of his cynicism is first of all Woman. British women, and Posthumus' "unparagon'd mistress" (80) are simply specific instances of the general law. "I make my wager rather against your confidence than her reputation. . . . I durst attempt it against any lady in the world" (110–13); but his barbs are personal, pointed and belittling and leave Posthumus little alternative than the mandatory chivalric response. "You may wear her in title yours; but you know strange fowl light upon neighbouring ponds" (88–9); "With five times so much conversation, I should get ground of your fair mistress" (103–4); "If you buy ladies' flesh at a million a dram, you cannot preserve it from tainting. But I see you have some religion in you, that you fear" (134–7).

There is no question about the provocation. The question that the scene raises is Posthumus' response. For what is, after all, the expected knightly procedure? Surely in such circumstances a man would challenge the slanderer, even the mere doubter of his mistress's honour, to a duel without further ado. It is himself, as against his adversary, that he would put to the test, not his inviolate lady. The scene itself reminds us of this in its reference to the previous occasion, and Philario, nervously attempting to allay the tension: "Let us leave here, gentlemen" (99), "Gentlemen, enough of this. It came in too suddenly; let it die as it was born, and I pray you be better acquainted" (120–2), has clearly such an outcome in mind. Instead of the "the arbiterment of swords" (49), however, we have the taking of the wager, which places the onus of proof upon the lady, and makes Posthumus' manly honor dependent, not upon an action of his, but upon an action, or nonaction, of hers. If Imogen prove faithless, "I am no further your enemy; she is not worth our debate" (159–60); but the whole chivalric point, surely, is to maintain at sword's point his *belief* in her faithfulness! If she is faithful, *then* he will punish Iachimo— "you shall answer me with your sword" (163). Both these alternatives take refuge in male bonds and relations in which, it seems, Posthumus shelters. The wager makes Imogen a mere object through which a bond with Iachimo is cemented: either he will become his friend, no woman between them, or his chastiser, again man to man. The wager reflects an inner question, the possibility of which the text has already insinuated into our minds: shall he (can he?) be a man among men, or a man to a woman?

If Iachimo finds her unassailable, and so not only of supreme worth but also manifestly devoted to Posthumus, this will flatter Posthumus' self-esteem; but what if the cunning, cynical Italian succeeds in gaining possession of "her dearest bodily part" (150), in performing, in other words, as Posthumus' proxy? Does the wager (rather than a duel) fulfill some inner need or desire of Posthumus himself? Is there a secret complicity between inveigler and inveigled?

What for that matter, if Cloten, master of all he surveys in England, gets possession of Imogen? These two are both assailants upon Imogen's chastity, would-be performers of her lover's role, and they are diametrically opposed, sophisticated, cunning, gallant and coarse lout, Queen's son though he be. They are clearly antithetical doubles. If there is an element of cultural comment in the mimetic aspect of their representation—English provincial against Italianate rogue—this remains marginal in the play as a whole. On the other hand the antithesis resonates throughout the whole play and acquires an organizing force when we can see it as in some way significantly related to Posthumus himself. Such a relation has been proposed by Murray Schwartz, building skillfully upon Freud's analysis of "The Universal Tendency to Debasement in the Sphere of Love."

Iachimo and Cloten, he says, "represent two related obsessions of a Renaissance personality burdened with the idealization and worship of women and seeking to establish a stable relationship between platonic sublimation and crude sexual expression." Both are "aspects or projections of Posthumus' psyche" which is "in tense and precarious balance" between alternative sexual modes (1976, 231). "By following Posthumus carefully through the play we can identify the dream-like logic (the logic of displacement, condensation, substitution, multiple symbolization) which underlies its sometimes confusing, over-sophisticated surface," and discover in him "the tyranny of the superego which would split the psyche into diametric opposites, one part that worships and another that defiles" (236).

We can interpret the play's psychomachia, then, as an inhibition of desire on Posthumus' part which is exhibited in extremely subtle ways through the two proxy suitors, the fastidious Iachimo and the unspeakable Cloten. The following account of this representation of inner conflict owes much to Schwartz' explication, though I do not follow him completely, either in detail or in respect to his conclusions.[5]

Cloten is introduced as early as Act I, scene ii in all his gross, rank, brute libidinality. Pretending to machismo, he is derided by his attendant lords with a flattery the irony of which is so palpable that only a Cloten-fool could miss it. We meet him again immediately before the bedroom scene, when his malodorous presence and his phallic/martial non-exploits are called attention to: "a pox on't! I had rather not be so noble as I am. They dare not fight with me because of the Queen my mother. Every Jack slave hath his bellyful of fighting, and I must go up and down like a cock that nobody can match" (II.i.18–22). Cloten, says Murray Schwartz, is "unadulterable phallic aggression" (1976, 222), a "personification of infantile fixations" (226); "Cloten represents. . . . uncontrolled phallic wishes that seek their objects relentlessly and without the least regard for otherness" (223). However, Cloten's sexuality is not sheer animal lust, or uninhibited libido. It is disowned by a constant defensive meiosis. The lexis with which he is associated is drawn from a "south-fog" (II.iii.131) of cloacal, noisome and obscene imagery. As Schwartz puts it, "He embodies the belief that sexuality defiles its object and drags chastity through the mire" (225). Cloten and Iachimo are not simply two rival evils laying siege to Imogen's integrity and virtue, but secret sharers in the psyche of the absent Posthumus for whom they substitute, and it is this that gives the two personae and the psychomachia they articulate its particular depth and interest. Both Cloten and his counterpart Iachimo ("Cloten in civilised dress," as Schwartz puts it, 227) represent isolated and split-off parts of an ambivalent and unintegrated personality, the one "arrogant piece of flesh," pure sexual drive, "the rebellion of a codpiece" (225); the other, pure, aim-inhibited fantasy as exhibited in the exquisite aestheticism of the bedroom scene.

Cloten, intent upon serenading the object of his desire, is nakedly lewd: "I am advis'd to give her music a'mornings; they say it will penetrate. . . . If you can penetrate her with your fingering, so; we'll try with tongue too" (II.iii.11–15). The aubade opens the scene which follows Iachimo's bedroom visit. The contrast could hardly be more extreme. The aubade is itself readable "from above" and "from below": as pretty Ovidian myth or, through its flying, its rising, its steeds watering at the springs of chaliced flowers, its winking Mary-buds that begin to ope their eyes, as veiled coitus. It is ironic in that no night of love has in fact been enjoyed; but it sharpens our perception that in fantasy one indeed has. The "fingering" and "tonguing" of Cloten has its marvelously imagined counterpart in Iachimo's soliloquy at Imogen's bedside.

Iachimo's virtuoso performance at his first meeting with Imogen gives us notice of his talent for verbalizing fantasy, for enlisting primary process imagery in the eliciting of sexual excitement:

> Had I this cheek
> To bathe my lips upon; this hand, whose touch
> (Whose every touch) would force the feeler's soul
> To th'oath of loyalty; this object, which
> Takes prisoner the wild motion of mine eye,
> Firing it only here; should I (damn'd then)
> Slaver with lips as common as the stairs
> That mount the Capitol (I.vi.99–106)

Somatic evocations of bodily sensations and excitations are aroused and disclaimed by the careful web of denigration of Posthumus and the "shes" that, he insinuates, Posthumus is "vaulting" in Rome: the sluts, the tomboys, the boiled stuff, the garbage that "Should make desire vomit emptiness, / Not so allured to feed" (45–6). It is the rhetoric of a maestro, but whom is it persuading? The audience is in the know at this point and must experience a species of split response, being partly persuaded as a real Imogen might have been persuaded, and partly persuaded only of the virtuosity of Iachimo. This means that the rhetoric itself is an object of attention and not a transparent medium, that the textuality (or fictionality) of the characters is not for a moment forgotten. This is an important point because it is what enables us to move about within the fictional space from one implied consciousness, or unconsciousness, to another.

We have no way of knowing whether his climactic ploy:

> Should he make me
> Live, like Diana's priest, betwixt cold sheets,
> Whiles he is vaulting variable ramps,
> In your despite, upon your purse—revenge it.
> I dedicate myself to your sweet pleasure (132–6)

is an inadvertent overreaching from which he adroitly extricates himself, or a part of his manipulative strategy. Nor can we know whether the trunk trick is a brilliant improvisation or, again, the culminating move in a premeditated masterplan; but we know that we are watching a game of cat and mouse. Nevertheless we are as manipulated as Imogen, who rejoices to take the trunk of jewels associated with Posthumus into the protection of her very bedchamber; we are as surprised as she would have been had she awoken, when Iachimo steps out of the trunk. The impact of the stage effect is therefore extremely shocking and partakes of that moment of disorientation often experienced upon waking from a dream when one is not yet able to distinguish between the oneiric and the real. It is as if the distancing fictional frame had collapsed and Iachimo is suddenly "real," really there or real in our minds, and this undoubtedly plays its part in creating the peculiarly intense effect of the passage which follows.

Iachimo would rather poison Posthumus' mind than possess Imogen's body. So he does not touch her. He denies himself the kiss which he projects onto the "rubies unparagoned" of her lips: "How dearly they do't!" (II.ii.17–18). "Doing," however, is far more than kissing in the imagery which follows. If we allow the language to work its will upon us we will perceive how Iachimo savors every moment of a fantasized sexual act. He begins with the invocation of Tarquin, relishing the latter's menacing tread: "Our Tarquin thus / Did softly press the rushes ere he waken'd / The chastity he wounded" (12–14). Desire is concentrated in an intensity of seeing, a lust of the eyes. The phallic flame of the taper is itself a voyeur as it "Bows toward her, and would under-peep her lids" (19–20); the bracelet (an upward displacement) is removed with ease—it is "As slippery as the Gordian knot was hard" (34); the climax, which has brought so many empathetic critics to a similar exalted state, engages a number of primal desires in its minutely observed image. The "crimson drops / I'th' bottom of a cowslip" (38–9), defloration in an innocently pastoral mask, is transferred to the mole upon her breast, redoubling fantasied pleasure. The soliloquy closes with an orgasm—a rape—completed: "the leaf's turn'd down / Where Philomel gave up" (45–6), and Iachimo, brought out of his trance by the striking clock (51), returns to the trunk with a gnawing sense of guilt.

Iachimo shrewdly exploits vicarious fantasy when he returns with his report, first of her bedchamber "where I confess I slept not" (II.iv.67), with its tapestry of Cleopatra "when she met her Roman / And Cydnus swelled above the banks" (70–1), its chimney piece of "Chaste Dian bathing" (81–2), its winking Cupid andirons, and finally the mole in its "delicate lodging" beneath her breast, which, he says, he kissed, to the enhancement of an appetite just sated (137–8). Posthumus is sexually aroused by the account. His bitter "Spare your arithmetic, never count the turns" (142) is vividly obscene, as is the tell-tale condensation of images in the rosy "pudency" (is the lady blushing? or is the sweet view another rosy site?) in his succeeding soliloquy:

> Me of my lawful pleasure she restrain'd
> And pray'd me oft forbearance; did it with
> A pudency so rosy the sweet view on't
> Might well have warm'd old Saturn, that I thought her
> As chaste as unsunn'd snow. (II.v.9–13)

Just as he "sees" that rosy "pudency" so he "sees" the "full-acorned" boar which "Cried 'O!' and mounted" (16–17), an image in which high feeding and high sexuality coalesce under the pressure of the imagined scene.

Posthumus, we perceive, is precipitated into his Cloten self, his unrecon-
structed, for him demeaning sensuality, by Iachimo's machinations. The bracelet is a basilisk—a Medusa's head—that kills him to look on; the metonymic
mole a "stain, as big as hell can hold" (II.iv.140); and in savage reaction he
will "tear her limb-meal!" (147), obliterating, in his misogynistic outburst, the
threat, and magnet, that is "the woman's part" (II.v.20). "The woman's part" is,
in analytic terminology, overdetermined. It is the "dearest bodily part" which
his exacerbated fantasy has "seen"; it is the maternal half of procreation which
he would repudiate: "Is there no way for men to be, but women / Must be
half-workers?" (1–2) and upon which he projects all falsities and evils, including his own sense of inauthenticity: his father was, must have been, absent
when he "was stamped," when "some coiner with his tools / Made [him] a
counterfeit" (5); and it is, as the woman's part in him—sex, his own repressed
sexuality, his own fear of sexual inadequacy, his sexual jealousy—for which he
blames women and from which he recoils in rage:

> I'll write against them,
> Detest them, curse them, yet 'tis greater skill
> In a true hate to pray they have their will:
> The very devils cannot plague them better. (32–5)

Finally, in the letter which informs Pisanio that "Thy mistress . . . hath
play'd the strumpet in my bed" (III.iv.21–2), Posthumus, in a perverse, self-
contaminating turn, incorporates the woman's part. "Thy mistress hath play'd
the strumpet in my bed: the testimonies whereof lies bleeding in me." It is he
who is the violated virgin since he cannot be the violator that in his present
sexual violence he would wish to be.

To illuminate the play's psychomachia from the side of the triad Posthumus, Iachimo, Cloten, however, is to default on half the story. There is
another side to the inner conflict in Act 11 which is plotted through the
opposite aspect of the triangle—Imogen, Iachimo, Cloten. The relations can
be diagramed:

Iachimo

Imogen   Posthumus

Cloten

These symmetries invite assessment of the protagonists as mirror images
of each other. Both are ideal objects to each other; both are victims; both take
flight and both seek rehabilitation (literally) in other clothing; and not only

Posthumus, but also Imogen, we very soon discover, is in subtle tension or disharmony with her sexuality.

We may have already noticed that Imogen, the fiercely rejected daughter ("Nay, let her languish / A drop of blood a day, and being aged / Die of this folly!" (I.i.156–8)) of a possessive father, chafes at the constraints of being a woman. Hearing of the near-fight between Posthumus and Cloten she says,

> I would they were in Afric both together,
> Myself by with a needle, that I might prick
> The goer-back. (167–9)

This is odd considering that the "goer-back," according to Pisanio, was Posthumus himself, and therefore betrays a certain vexation in this abandoned bride. Her reference to her husband as "My supreme crown of grief. . . . Had I been thief-stol'n, / As my two brothers, happy!" (I.vi.4–6) has already been noted. . . . Imogen is ardent and loving, and not about to admit to any defect in her beloved, but her tongue betrays her.

She is herself hard-pressed. Not only does she remain alone, in virtual imprisonment, in the absence of her lover, beset by the coarse lout she detests as much as she detests his mother, but she is verbally assaulted by the man who comes to her as her husband's friend.

We note her spirited resistance to Iachimo's innuendos in the testing scene, and her repudiation of him when he gives himself away; but it is his giveaway that has saved her. "My lord, I fear, / Has forgot Britain" (I.vi.112–13) she has just said, dismayed despite herself. It is this perhaps that accounts for the eagerness with which, appeased by Iachimo's retraction, she takes the trunk into custody into her own bedchamber. However, there is, we are invited to infer, another reason. The precious trunk contains jewels purchased by Posthumus: its contents stand therefore, as nearly as any object may, for his bodily presence. It is both in longing and to make amends that she wishes it so close.

Imogen, in the bedroom scene, is an inert, sleeping presence, the object of Iachimo's fantasy, but the references to time which set off and frame Iachimo's soliloquy, mark off a timeless space of fantasy, or dream, for Imogen too. She has been reading for three hours, we learn, before she falls asleep. She prays for protection, as she puts her book aside, from "fairies and the tempters of the night" (II.ii.9); and when we discover at what episode her reading terminated—in the tale of Tereus, "where Philomel gave up" (46)—we can see why. Wedded, but unbedded, abandoned, in effect, by her husband, her marriage proscribed and herself rejected by her father, beset like Penelope by unwanted suitors, the story of Philomel and Tereus objectifies ambivalent fear and excitement.

In the next scene she is the victim of Cloten's gross attentions, no less unsettling than were Iachimo's crafty manipulations. She has also lost her bracelet. So, understandably, at Cloten's curse, "The south-fog rot him!" (II. iii.131), she momentarily loses her composure; but her vehement comparison is more expressive than perhaps she, the imagined persona, is aware:

> His mean'st garment
> That ever hath but clippt his body, is dearer
> in my respect than all the hairs above thee,
> Were they all made such men. (133–6)

What is a man's meanest garment? The train of thought picks up from Cloten's talk about Posthumus' "beggary," but the train of feeling, we intuit, arises elsewhere. This garment "clippt his body." A man's homely underwear could presumably fit the bill as his meanest garment, and it is also that which "clips" his body closest. Read thus, the otherwise entirely obscure leap to Cloten's tonsorial style (or wig?) becomes explicable. The displacement upwards of the body-image is a protection from the recognition, which it also divulges, of a lively desire. Just such a displacement, common in dream language, this time from sexual to aural penetration occurs in her response to Pisanio's embassy: "Speak thick / (Love's counsellor should fill the bores of hearing, / To th' smothering of the sense). . . . Tell me how Wales was made so happy as / T' inherit such a haven" (III.ii.56–62, passim). Her mingling of ardour, impatience and trepidation, touching in itself, is given a further dimension when we take in the deeper resonances.

Cloten, thick-witted in all but his own monolithic concerns, gets the humiliating point about the clothes, as is made clear in the sequel when he sends for Posthumus' clothes in which he will pursue the pair to Milford Haven:

> Even there, thou villain Posthumus, will I kill thee. . . . . She said
> upon a time (the bitterness of it I now belch from my heart) that
> she held the very garment of Posthumus in more respect than
> my noble and natural person, together with the adornment of my
> qualities. With that suit upon my back will I ravish her; first kill
> him, and in her eyes; there shall she see my valor, which will then
> be a torment to her contempt. He on the ground, my speech of
> insultment ended on his dead body, and when my lust hath din'd
> (which, as I say, to vex her I will execute in the clothes that she

so praised) to the court I'll knock her back, foot her home again.
(III.v.131–46, passim)

"O for a horse with wings!" Imogen says, when Posthumus' letter summons her to Milford Haven (III.ii.48). And when Pisanio assures her that
they can cover no more than a score of miles "twixt sun and sun" (68): "Why,
one that rode to's execution, man, / Could never go so slow" (70–1). This is
patent dramatic irony, of course. Pisanio has already read Posthumus' murder
letter, and Imogen will hear of it before she gets to her heaven-haven; but if
nothing is accidental in the world of the mind then the uttering of such a
comparison must indicate the presence of an underlying dread. The manner
in which this passionate and high-spirited girl—who has defied her father's
fury, who struggles, alone, to resolve the ambivalence of untried sexuality,
suffering the absence of her lover with some accusatory vexation, however
unacknowledged—responds to the outrage of her husband's misconception
of her becomes thus poignantly understandable:

> False to his bed? What is it to be false?
> To lie in watch there and to think on him?
> To weep 'twixt clock and clock? If sleep charge nature,
> To break it with a fearful dream of him,
> And cry myself awake? (III.iv.40–4)

Outraged and bewildered, her defense against his accusations takes the form
of an accusatory injury against herself: she begs Pisanio to kill her—to do his
master's bidding—with an image of mutilation, of positive dismemberment:

> Poor I am stale, a garment out of fashion,
> And for I am richer than to hang by, th' walls,
> I must be ripp'd. To pieces with me! (51–3)

This is a turning inward of her anger and her anguish. She sees herself
a hunted or trapped creature, a sacrificial lamb or deer, turns feminine sexual
submission into masochistic punishment as she tosses away the protective
wad of Posthumus' letters in her bosom and invites the sword's penetration:
"Obedient as the scabbard" (80). Her first defense against the mortification
of Posthumus' treatment of her is a literal mortifying of herself—a mort of
the deer, so to speak.

However, Imogen, possessed of remarkable resilience, recovers. Even
before Pisanio's suggestion of the page disguise, she has taken heart, and
determined, in the first place, not to return to the court:

No court, no father, nor no more ado
With that harsh, noble, simple nothing,
That Cloten, whose love suit hath been to me
As fearful as a siege. . . . .
Hath Britain all the sun that shines? day? night?
Are they not but in Britain? (131–7)

Her response to her plight, like Posthumus' to his, but with opposite effect, is also to reject "the woman's part" in her, to "forget to be a woman" (154). She embraces Pisanio's idea of the journey to Italy with enthusiasm, is "almost a man already" (166–7), and will "abide it with a prince's courage" (183–4); but Imogen's transvestite fantasy solves nothing.

First of all, footsore and weary, she discovers that "a man's life is a tedious one" (III.vi.l), as she remarks with a wry humor. However, it is her hermaphrodite membership in the reconstituted family of Belarius which makes clear that her flight from her sex will never do. Not only is her real sex only partly concealed—the brothers clearly fall in love with the feminine quality of her beauty (much as does Orsino with Cesario's): "Were you a woman, youth, / I should woo hard" (68–9)—but also the family likeness between the three is, we infer, only partly concealed. Unavailable to conscious knowledge it is evidently unconsciously registered. For Imogen the vigorous masculinity of the peerless twain is extremely attractive but what it precipitates is a wishful fantasy about her lost brothers, which she invokes to mitigate the defaulting of Posthumus. "Would . . . they / Had been my father's sons" (75–6) she thinks, for then, no longer sole heiress to her father's crown (nor sole object of his possessive love)—her "prize" would have been less and so "more equal ballasting" to Posthumus, and their love might have fared better (76–7). As it is, rejected and calumniated she reaffirms that she would rather be a man in their company than a woman to the false Leonatus.

The audience, knowing what it knows, perceives this encounter synoptically. What is (and is not) being recognized by the brothers is Imogen's true gender. What is not (and yet is) being recognized by all three is their kinship. The love which springs up between them is therefore a composite of elements: narcissistic, erotic and familial, a volatile quantity which cannot recognize itself or disentangle its objects.

The rural retreat in Wales is the "green world" or other place which in Shakespearean comedy is liberating and restorative;[6] but it is a retreat—from maturation; a return to infancy, or even beyond, to the shelter of a cave/womb. Belarius is a mother/father—he was a tree "whose boughs did bend with fruit" until the "storm or robbery" which "shook down [his] mellow hangings . . . and left [him] bare to weather" (III.iii.61–4). The siblings are androgynous, or sexless—Fidele sings like an angel, and cooks like one too; they all, in fact, cook and keep house like women, though the boys are hunters too. This denial of adult differentiation is, on the one hand, gratifying, healing, a wishful undoing, but the play keeps a stern and monitoring eye on it.

The retreat is glossed in the homilies of Belarius as a beneficent exchange of the sophistries and corruptions of the court for the archaic simplicities of nature, and his contempt for the gates of monarchs, which are "arched so high that giants may jet through / And keep their impious turbands on without / Good morrow to the sun" (5–7), is a detraction of masculine arrogance. It is subverted by the aspiration of the boys to live the life of the "full-winged eagle" rather than that of the "sharded beetle" (20–1), and by Belarius' own approval of their "wild" violence, which he sees as evidence of an "invisible instinct" of royalty (IV.ii.177ff). They are precariously poised, in their immaturity, between the noble and the savage; and, all unawares, between innocence and incest since the eruption into their lives of Fidele. The Belarius family romance—designed to "bar [the king] of succession" (III.iii.102)—represents a barren wish. Belarius' is a fantasy family whose childlike nondifferentiation is regressive.

Back at the British court sexual roles are also, in their own way, fruitlessly and damagingly inverted. Cymbeline is patently reluctant to rise against the imperial father figure Caesar, who knighted him and under whom he spent his youth. Patriotic self-assertion is left to the Queen and her son, whose joint monopolization of the masculine virtues is rendered in interestingly characteristic ways. Cloten, crude as ever, announces that "we will nothing pay / For wearing our own noses" (III.i.13–14). The Queen describes the British isles as a *hortus inclusus* ("Neptune's park," within its "salt-water girdle" in Cloten's description (80)), a space normally feminine in the symbology of landscapes, but here fortified and lethal:

> ribb'd and pal'd in
> With oaks unscalable and roaring waters,
> With sands that will not bear your enemies' boats,
> But suck them up to th' topmast. (19–22)

Britain's heirs, cavemen in Wales, are mothered by a man, Britain itself is kinged by a woman, who, if she has her way and her wish for the speedy demise of both Imogen and her father, will soon in fact "have the placing of the British crown" upon her son's head (III.v.65). The play's central Act has brought the drama to an imminent crisis of intrigue at court, and war over the tribute money. In Belarius' other isle Cloten closes in upon the fugitive Imogen. Appropriately, at the outset of Act IV Fidele, succumbing to grief for her lost love, falls ill.

In Shakespearean tragic structure we regularly find protagonists in Act IV facing a great void, an annihilation of the values which have sustained them. Deprived of their objects of love or faith or hope, they experience despair, so that possible remedy, tantalizingly just within reach, is occluded from their view, or, if perceived, is snatched away by the circumstances which have swept beyond control. In his comic structures, Act IV initiates the remedial phase of the narrative, exorcizing precedent errors and follies by maximilizing them to the point of exhaustion. In *Cymbeline*, the most intricately interlocked of the tragicomedies, both vectors coexist, and are synchronized in the play's most phantasmagoric event—the mock death of Fidele. In terms of form the bizarre and lurid events in Wales mark the concatenation of the two contradictory genres in a grotesque indeterminacy of tragic and comic effects. In terms of fantasy they mark a turning point in the working through of the deep conflicts the play articulates.

Imogen, heartsick, takes the potion given her by Pisanio in the belief that it is remedial, which it is, the malignant will of the Queen having been outwitted by Cornelius, her physician, who exchanged her poisonous brew for a harmless narcotic. Only Cornelius, however, knows this. It enables the tragicomic transformation of grave and serious events into restorative and gratifying ends. Had it been the poison the Queen intended it to be, Imogen's taking it, on advice from the good Pisanio, would have constituted the fatal error in a tragic sequence of ironic reversals and disasters. As it is, it constitutes the mock deception which brings about a sequence of harmless (though painful) errors, mistaken identities and confusions, which will issue, despite the harm already caused, in a benign resolution. It is the cause of the (apparent) death which the play, as comedy, will surmount, while at the same time it is the cause that the death *is* only apparent, a deathlike trance. It thus provides for a playing out and working through, in imagination, of the despairing or destructive urge which drags against the play's reconstructive thrust.

Cloten, hot-foot on Imogen's track, vicious in his retaliatory intent to kill Posthumus, ravish her and spurn her home to her father, is beheaded by Guiderius, and his "clotpole" sent down the stream "in embassy to his mother" (IV.ii.185) in a strange parody of pagan fertility rituals. As a consequence, the Queen, bereft, so to speak, of her male organ, declines and dies. This effectively does away with the evil ones, eliminating sadism and reincorporating it with its primal source, the voracious mother of infantile fantasy.

That Imogen, who was found in bed by Iachimo, is now found in her (death) bed with Cloten, reiterates the relationship of these two to her absent husband: the one representing the repressed libido in him, the other the repressive superego. Posthumus' next appearance, as we shall see, exhibits him with the violent Cloten-id elements in his personality entirely extinguished, and later he will rout Iachimo in single fight; but we shall return to Posthumus' fortunes presently.

In terms of the emotional dynamic of the play it is a melancholy course that is charted by the sequence from bedroom scene to burial scene. In the bedroom scene eroticism was deviant and devious, but alive. The bedroom scene was accompanied by the aubade, an accolade to love; the burial scene by the dirge, which welcomes death. This haunting lyric envisages a sublime indifference to reed as to oak, to both joy and moan, a placid acceptance of the dust to which golden lads and girls must come. Its desire is for death, for the cessation of being and of vicissitude, a "quiet consummation" devoutly to be wished. However, Imogen wakes bewildered from her drugged stupor to discover the headless body of Cloten/Posthumus beside her. "Limb-meal" she inventories her lover's body:

> I know the shape of's leg; this is his hand,
> His foot Mercurial, his Martial thigh,
> The brawns of Hercules; but his jovial face—
> Murther in heaven? (IV.ii.309–12)

Throwing herself upon the faceless, headless body she enacts an hysterical incorporation: she smears her cheek with the blood of the corpse, as if to die herself, or, in a gruesome fantasy realization of Elizabethan "dying," to match her maidenhead with the violated head of her lover.[7] In this "consummation" Eros is undone, overwhelmed, by Thanatos, its dark companion.

"I am nothing; or if not, / Nothing to be were better" (367–8) is Imogen's desolate reply to Lucius' question "What art thou?" (366) when he comes upon the scene at the graveside. It is just here that the countermovement to recovery is initiated. Fidele's head was to be laid to the east, we recall, in preparation, we now perceive, for just such a rebirth. "Wilt take thy chance with me? I will not say / Thou shalt be so well master'd, but be sure / No less belov'd" (382–4), Lucius says, and in response to her vulnerable epicene youthfulness insists that he would "rather father thee than master thee" (395). Imogen, dogged survivor, responds.

Posthumus' progress towards recovery begins with his conscience-stricken, grief-stricken soliloquy at the start of the play's final phase. This is our first meeting with Posthumus since his outburst of misogyny in Act II, scene v. Now he addresses the bloody cloth, evidence, as he believes, of Imogen's death. The great rage is killed in him, and there is a yearning for some form of expression for love, although he is still convinced of Imogen's "wrying":

> You married ones,
> If each of you should take this course, how many
> Must murther wives much better than themselves
> For wrying but a little!. . . . .
>   Gods, if you
> Should have ta'en vengeance on my faults, I never
> Had liv'd to put on this; so had you saved
> The noble Imogen to repent, and strook
> Me, wretch, more worth your vengeance. But alack,
> You snatch some hence for little faults; that's love,
> To have them fall no more. . . .
>   I'll . . .
>   suit myself
> As does a Britain peasant; so I'll fight
> Against the part I come with; so I'll die
> For thee, O Imogen, even for whom my life
> Is every breath a death (V.i.2–27, passim)

Is there equivocation in "the part I come with" (we recall "the woman's part in him" so bitterly denounced); it is at all events the sadistic, revengeful Cloten part of him which is here repudiated. Later, he routs Iachimo whose "manhood" has been "taken off" by "the heaviness and guilt within [his] bosom (V.ii.1–2). Neither of the remorseful pair is aware of the other's identity, and there seems little sense, plot-wise, in the dumbshow fight which is superfluous to the conduct of the war and the rescue of the King, the matter at issue at this point in the story. All the more inviting, therefore, is it to see the victory as a symbolic defeat of the Iachimo within.

It is the rescue of the King, however, which serves as focus of the action. It is anticipated by the two boys, given in dumbshow, and then again in Posthumus' vividly detailed account. Three times during the sequence the setting of the heroic feat is described: in a narrow lane (ditched and walled with turf), an old man and two boys (the British forces having retreated in disarray) are defending the King from the oncoming Roman host, when Posthumus joins them. Why the triple insistence? Battle at a narrow entry is, psychoanalytic findings inform us, a classic symbolization of oedipal conflict. In the context of other subliminal recoveries in this phase of the play, the episode reads like an oedipal conflict reversed, or resolved. No father is killed at a crossroads, or maternal portal, but a king is saved, and by his own sons, together with their other (supposed) father, with Posthumus, the unknown soldier, the foster-son, as partner. The text is underscoring its message, but for Posthumus further realizations are necessary before the catastrophic splits in his personality can be truly healed. Isolated, unknown and bereaved, he is still in despair. His oscillating changes of dress from Roman to British signify that he is a man without an identity, rudderless, directionless, deprived of the will to live. Only death offers a surcease to the pain of loss and the agony of conscience; but he cannot find death "where [he] did hear him groan, / Nor feel him where he strook" (V.iii.69–70). The more daringly and fearlessly he fights, the more invulnerable he seems.

When he is captured, therefore, this time in Roman clothing, he welcomes his imprisonment, begging the "good gods" who he welcomes his imprisonment, begging the "good gods" who "coin'd" his life not to extend his torment, not to be "appeased," like "temporal fathers" by his sorrow, and looks forward to his execution with an eagerness which makes the Gaoler remark "Unless a man would marry a gallows and beget young gibbets, I never saw one so prone" (V.iv.198–9). It is at this point that the death-courting Posthumus has a transforming dream.

The departure from blank verse for the dream and the theophany embedded in it have caused much critical agitation[8] which has simply obscured the insight the dream's substance provides into Posthumus' state of mind. The dream, for Posthumus, is a transparent wish-fulfillment. The parental presences which materialize in the dream are solacing, comforting, approving; "our son is good" is the burden of their sayings. He fell asleep grief and guilt stricken, invoking the image of the injured Imogen, craving for the punishment, and the relief, of death. In the dream he is embraced, pitied, exonerated by parents and siblings alike. When he awakes to the pain of the loss of this oneiric family, he is nevertheless imbued with a sense of a "golden chance," of having been "steep'd in favours" (V.iv.131–2); and although he is still absolute for death even after the dream, and unable to interpret the oracular message, the fantasy of recuperation points to its possibility.

Both Imogen and Posthumus thus experience an annihilating despair, their recovery from which is staged in parallel fashion: through the second-chance gift of protective parents. However, their rehabilitation will not be completely realized until the climactic moment of the blow the unrecognized Imogen receives at Posthumus' hand when she intercedes, in order to reveal herself, at the height of his lament for the woman he has wronged and lost. It is a dramatic moment, but it is more than a mere *coup de théâtre*. This acting out of aggression immediately undone by recognition and forgiveness is therapeutic. The blow is an uninhibited action, spontaneous, unconstrained, passionate, and this is a capacity that his masculinity needs as much as her femininity desires. The shock, moreover, functions for both like a clearing of the air, a clearance of debt or a lovers' quarrel, defusing unconscious resentments which could fester and obstruct, functioning to liberate him from his fear of sexual inadequacy, her from her fear of sexual surrender.

What he says as he hits her is pregnant with dramatic irony bred of all the blindnesses there have been between them, and within them:

Shall's have a play of this? Thou scornful page,
There lie thy part. (V.v.228–9)

This is the last time we shall hear that telling little word "part." Fragmentation and self-division are abrogated in the image Posthumus uses when the two at last embrace: "Hang there like fruit, my soul, / Till the tree die!" (263–4). It is an image which is impossible to dismantle: for we cannot tell whether his own soul or she herself is the anaphoric antecedent of "my soul," nor whether "there" is the space within his embracing arms or hers. Does he imagine Imogen hanging like fruit upon his fatherly support? Or does he imagine himself hanging upon her maternal support like a fruit which need never (till the tree die) be detached? This culminating moment annuls the dirge, offers fruit for the latter's dust. Yet it contains its own knowledge of finitude, despite its fantasy of merger and completion of self in other, for even the tree will, one day, die.

The soothsayer's culminating account, to Cymbeline, of his vision of peace is analogous in its mixing of gender. The eagle-Caesar is indeterminately male and female, so therefore also is radiant Cymbeline in this mythological union of their powers:

the Roman eagle,
From south to west on wing soaring aloft,
Lessen'd herself and in the beams o'th' sun
So vanish'd; which foreshow'd our princely eagle,
Th'imperial Caesar, should again unite
His favor with the radiant Cymbeline,
Which shines here in the west. (470–6)

It is a strange, even monstrous valedictory emblem for a very strange play. Have we, with the aid of the psychoanalytic insights, made sense of it? Of any part of it? Has our attempt to "follow the path of the signifier," and to tell the other story of *Cymbeline* thrown light into the shadowy reaches of the textual unconscious which was our quarry?

The play has been inundated by fantasies of dispersed and reassembled families, parents, siblings, marriage partners; of split and recuperated identities; of "lopp'd branches, which, being dead many years, shall after revive, be jointed to the old stock, and freshly grow" (438–40). Implicit in all these has been an urgent will to transform the forces making for death and dissolution into a reaffirmation of procreative life. The *pater familias* of Act V, full of affection and happiness, joyful "mother to the birth of three" (369) is manifestly not the Cymbeline, the "*nom (non) du père,*" of the beginning, as destructive in his tyrannical possessiveness as he was submissive to the wife who deceived and enthralled him, and as patently a projection of oedipal fantasy as was his poison-queen of an earlier infantile stage of development.

It is no doubt the sense of an unresolved strangeness that causes Murray Schwartz to judge the play "a failure"—"a play with a broken ego" (1976, 270), but this is because he focuses upon Posthumus as a case study in neurosis—Shakespeare's, and that of "the dominant ego of his age, polarised in its conception of sexual identity" (282) and its attitude to feminine power. "Shakespeare," he says, "has not yet found the psychic courage to admit that the fears and aggressions he evokes in *Cymbeline* reside in a father, and that their object is an unconsciously harbored mother imago" (283). This is absurd since either it postulates a Shakespeare who could only know what he knew by having undergone a course in the psychoanalytic theory of the Oedipus complex, or it does not remember that it was Shakespeare who wrote the play *Hamlet* some ten years before the composition of *Cymbeline.* Moreover, if it is a question of "psychic courage" in the probing of the inner life, I should think that *King Lear* alone should be sufficient evidence of Shakespeare's possession of that attribute. Not to mention *Coriolanus.*

Nevertheless we may still feel that there remains a gap in our perception of *Cymbeline.* The bits do not cohere. It stays fragmented in our minds, a bundle of lively, or lurid but disintegrated parts. The testing question with which this study began is whether we can close this gap, whether we can move through the Lacanian witticism from ellipse as textual gap to ellipse as transferential circuit in which text and reader can meet.

Fruitful in this respect is Charles Hofling's reminder that Shakespeare's mother died the year before *Cymbeline* is generally held to have been composed, and that in the same year a daughter was born to his own recently married favorite daughter. The following year Shakespeare returned to Stratford, and to his wife, after the twenty-year absence in London which followed the birth of his third child (1965, 133ff.). This is suggestive; and taken in tandem with the obsessively repetitive imagery of severance, fragmentation and recuperation precipitates a concluding insight.

Freud, in his reflections upon the Triple Goddess—the three significant women figures in a man's life—exhibits an odd amnesia. When he expands upon the story of the three caskets it is mother, wife and burying earth that he names, forgetting a fourth possibility.[9] Shakespeare's romances are, in effect, a riposte. The beloved, thaumaturgic daughters of these last plays supplement Freud's death-dominated triad. The three significant women in a man's life in these late plays are mother, wife and daughter, new life-bringer, who can reverse, at least in fantasy, the decline into death.

Consider the "death" of Fidele/Imogen. Belarius' "ingenious instrument" (IV.ii.186) is sounded for the first time since the death of the boys' supposed mother when Fidele dies, and she is to be buried beside the latter's grave. In her mock death she takes the place of Euriphile who took the place of the boys' real mother (who was also her own), whose place was taken by the deathly Queen mother. Lucius announces that no master had a page "so kind . . . so tender . . . so nurse-like" (V.v.86–8). She is not only herself symbolically reborn, she is the cause rebirth is in others, that is, in Cymbeline, the absent, occulted father, proxy for his author, the productions of whose imagination are all splinters of the self, of "His Majesty the Ego."[10] In this view the motivating, generating fantasy, or perplexity, of the play is located in the figure of the King, and it is this that enables us to move from Lacan's ellipse as a gap in the text, to the ellipse as a circuit connecting text and reader. If we unbind the text in this way, if we see Posthumus as a proxy for Cymbeline in the latter's absence, just as Iachimo and Cloten were proxies for Posthumus in his absence, and behind the whole series of figures a troubled author whose preoccupations the foregrounded stories screen, and while screening reveal, we can suddenly see the whole fable in a new light.

It is a father's deeply repressed desire for his daughter that is relayed through Posthumus, hence he is shackled and hampered in the conduct of his love. Hence the "killing" of Imogen, sham though it be, and the necrophilia of that nightmarish scene. Hence her rescue by a benign, protective father figure, whom she in turn "nurses," as Lucius makes a point of telling us. Yet in the recognition scenes there are still painful resonances: Imogen, it seems, deserts her "father" Lucius; Belarius reexperiences the loss of the children, "two of the sweet'st companions in the world" (V.v.349) that Cymbeline lost. The severing and reestablishing of parent/grown-child relationships is an arduous and troubled work of transformation, of the dislodging and redeployment of invested emotions, as we may learn from Shakespeare's dramas, if not from life. It is the work of late maturity, no benign retirement, but fraught with layer upon layer of old anxieties and hostilities, layer upon layer of new rivalries and jealousies. This is the work of the oneiric imagination throughout the late plays; and it is to this seedbed of Shakespeare's romances that *Cymbeline* can give us access.

Notes

1. Bertrand Evans, *Shakespeare's Comedies* (Oxford, Clarendon Press, 1960), has shown how the discrepancy between audience knowledge and character

knowledge is greater in *Cymbeline* than in any other of Shakespeare's plays. The characters are kept more ignorant and of more essential matters than anywhere else. Hence the accumulation of discoveries in Act V.

2. See Gilbert D. Chaitin, "The Representation of Logical Relations in Dreams and the Nature of Primary Process," *Psychoanalysis and Contemporary Thought*, II (1978); Pinchas Noy, "A Revision of the Psychoanalytic Theory of Primary Process," *Int. Jnl. Psycho-Analysis*, 50 (1969); and "Symbolism and Mental Representation," *Annual of Psychoanalysis*, I (1973) for useful accounts of primary and secondary processes of thought.

3. Most famous of the Victorian adorers is Swinburne who calls Imogen "the very crown and flower of all her father's daughters . . . woman above all Shakespeare's women . . . the immortal godhead of womanhood" (*A Study of Shakespeare*, 1880).

4. See Richard Levin, *The Multiple Plot in English Renaissance Drama* (Chicago, University of Chicago Press, 1971).

5. In general Schwartz' rigorously "Applied Psychoanalysis" is only partially successful. It suffers from an excessive orthodoxy which attempts to diagnose and schematize exhaustively in accordance with classic psychoanalytic terms and themes. And he tends to see Imogen exclusively as an object of the men's fantasies. "Shakespeare," he says, "forces Imogen to reenact regressive states we see in Cymbeline and Posthumus. . . . . In this inverted primal scene Imogen is the "man" who "dies" at the sight of the castrated body; she has become a surrogate for Posthumus, who is "killed" by the sight of the female genitals. The scene works to deny the masculine fantasy by expressing it in an utterly inverted way" (266).

6. See Ruth Nevo, *Comic Transformations in Shakespeare* (London, Methuen, 1980).

7. Cf. in *Measure for Measure*, IV.ii.1–5 and *Romeo and Juliet*, I.i.21–6.

8. Discussion of the problem and its implications for the question of authorship can be found in Nosworthy (1980, xxxvi–vii).

9. The omission may seem less surprising when one recalls that the Three Caskets essay (1913) does antedate by many years the loving care bestowed upon her ailing father by his "Anna-Antigone," as Freud called his own beloved daughter. See *Letters of Sigmund Freud, 1873–1939*, ed. Tania Stern and James Stern (New York, Basic Books, 1960), 424.

10. The phrase is Freud's in *Creative Writers and Daydreaming* (1908).

RENÉ GIRARD

The Crime and Conversion of
Leontes in The Winter's Tale

I

When we think of those phenomena in which mimicry is likely to play a role, we enumerate such things as dress, mannerisms, facial expressions, speech, stage acting, artistic creation, and so forth, but we never think of desire. Consequently, we see imitation in social life as a force for gregariousness and bland conformity through the mass reproduction of a few social models.

If imitation also plays a role in desire, if it contaminates our urge to acquire and possess, this conventional view, while not entirely false, misses the main point. Imitation does not merely draw people together, it pulls them apart. Paradoxically, it can do these two things simultaneously. Individuals who desire the same thing are united by something so powerful that, as long as they can share whatever they desire, they remain the best of friends; as soon as they cannot, they become the worst of enemies.

There are many ways in which Shakespeare's characters become involved in mimetic desire. The simplest one is to fall in love with the lover of your best friend, as Proteus does in *The Two Gentlemen of Verona*, or as the boys and girls do in *A Midsummer Night's Dream*. Shakespeare also created characters with a great appetite for the mimetic desire of their friends and associates, which they skillfully incite, such as Valentine in *The Two Gentlemen of Verona* or Troilus in *Troilus and Cressida*. These characters need the reinforcement

From *Religion and Literature* 22, nos. 2–3 (Summer–Autumn 1990): 193–219. Copyright ©
1990 by the Department of English, University of Notre Dame.

of a second desire similar to their own, and they turn their best friends into fierce enemies. Many of them are unaware of their responsibility in their own misfortune.

There is also a third kind of character who behaves very much like the second kind, but, instead of remaining blissfully ignorant of their own curious propensities, these characters become excessively suspicious of their innocent partners because they intensely distrust themselves. The most famous of these obsessively jealous characters is Othello, but there are other great examples, such as Claudio in *Much Ado About Nothing*, Posthumus in *Cymbeline*, and above all, Leontes, the protagonist of *The Winter's Tale*.

With no one at his side to poison his mind, this king of Sicilia comes close to destroying his entire family. His faithful wife of many years, Hermione, is selflessly devoted to him; his supposed rival, Polixenes, the king of Bohemia, is a perfectly loyal friend.

In Act I, ii, we watch the sudden transformation of Leontes into a wild beast. Contrary to what many critics say, this great scene contains all that is needed for a full understanding of this hero's jealousy.

After a nine month visit with Leontes and Hermione, Polixenes announces that he must return to his family and the affairs of Bohemia. Greatly distressed by this decision, Leontes begs his friend to stay at least a few more days. He is so desperately eager to keep Polixenes in Sicilia that he becomes incoherent and, most abruptly, even impolitely, he turns to Hermione who stands silently at his side:

> Tongue-tied our queen? speak you.
> (I, ii, 27)

The only "tongue-tied" character in this scene is Leontes himself. Knowing how persuasive his wife can be, he wishes that she had intervened without being asked. He is as dependent on her as he is on his friend and he feels that the two most important people in his life have betrayed him. Sensing his disarray, Hermione first tries to reassure him:

> I had thought, sir, to have held my peace until
> You had drawn oaths from him not to stay. You, sir,
> Charge him too coldly.
> (28–30)

She then proceeds to "charge" Polixenes in her own warm and friendly manner, without ever losing her dignity. Leontes is highly pleased. Twice he repeats "well said, Hermione."

Polixenes quickly yields to Hermione's entreaties and he decides to postpone his departure; Leontes is full of admiration and gratitude:

At my request he would not.
Hermione, my dearest, thou never spok'st
To better purpose.
    (87–89)

Hermione asks her husband if he really means this last statement. In a light-hearted way, he answers that, on one other occasion only, she spoke as well as she just did, on the day when she said "yes" to his marriage proposal. All she does after that is to *repeat* more or less what her husband has just said:

. . . . I have spoke to th' purpose twice:
The one, for ever earn'd a royal husband;
Th' other, for some while a friend.
    (106–108)

As she says these words, Hermione gives her hand to Polixenes. At this precise instant, Leontes feels overwhelmed with jealousy:

[Aside] Too hot, too hot!
To mingle friendship far, is mingling bloods.
I have *tremor cordis* on me: my heart dances,
But not for joy—not joy.
    (108–111)

Occurring as it does *in front of Leontes*, Hermione's display of affection for Polixenes cannot mean what the husband now wants it to mean. Leontes is aware of this and yet, he persists in his mad new belief. What is the cause of his sudden jealousy?

During his wife's conversation with Polixenes, Leontes had moved away and, being out of hearing, he shouted: "Is he won yet?", meaning Polixenes. In the following exchange, when she associated these two ideas, "earning a husband" and "earning a friend," Hermione simply borrowed Leontes' metaphor.

When Leontes sees that his wife *imitates* him, he is terrified. For nine long months, he had dreamed of a perfect triangular union with Polixenes and Hermione. The same close relationship should exist between these two, he felt, as he, Leontes, already entertained with each one separately. During the entire visit of his friend, he had sensed, on his part, some reticence toward his wife, and, on her part, some reticence toward his friend. He interpreted their mutual reserve as an implicit rebuke of himself; maybe he was disdained by his wife for choosing the wrong friend, disdained by his friend for choosing the wrong wife.

At the beginning of the scene, Leontes was still attempting a rapprochement between Polixenes and Hermione, still convinced of his failure. Hence his unhappiness with Polixenes' announcement of his departure, his irritation with Hermione for not spontaneously voicing her opposition. Then, all of a sudden, when he heard his wife echo his own words, this terribly insecure man changed his mind completely. He decided that his efforts had been successful after all, far too successful. His estimate of his own influence shifted from one extreme to the other.

Hermione has made Polixenes understand how important it is not to her but to her husband that his friend should stay a little longer, and Polixenes has bowed to her request. Leontes perceives very well this docility to his slightest wish, this tendency of both Hermione and Polixenes to turn into carbon copies of himself.

Leontes has been using his wife as his go-between with another man. Reflecting on this fact, he sees himself as a mimetic model quite different from the one he wanted to be, an involuntary Pandarus, driving his wife into the arms of his friend, driving his friend into the arms of his wife.

For nine long months, Leontes believes, he was *le cocu magnifique* and he, alone, did not know. Everybody must be making fun of him behind his back. When Camillo refuses to believe in the treachery of Hermione, Leontes concludes that he, too, must be part of the conspiracy:

> Camillo was his help in this, his pandar.
> (II, i, 46)

The king accuses his trusted counsellor of persevering in the role that he, the complacent husband, had mimetically invited him to play, by playing it in front of him.

The meaning of it all is first formulated by the same reliable Camillo, the man best informed of what his master is up to. Speaking to a startled Polixenes, he sums up Leontes' delusion in eight words:

> He thinks, nay, with all confidence he swears,
> As he had seen't, or *been an instrument*
> *To vice you to't*, that you have touch'd his queen
> Forbiddenly.
> (414–417; italics mine)

Leontes never said in so many words: "I myself planted an adulterous desire in the heart of my wife and of my friend," and the prudent Camillo presents his diagnosis as tentative but it is not conjectural in the slightest; it is fully confirmed both by Leontes at the end of this scene, and by Hermione at the beginning of Act III, when she defends herself against her husband's unjust accusation.

*   *   *

Let us take up Hermione first. What she says is entirely true and it vindicates her completely but it also reveals the element of perspicacity in Leontes' jealousy, the crucial point that the critics never see:

> For Polixenes,
> With whom I am accus'd, I do confess
> I lov'd him as in honour he requir'd,
> With such a kind of love as might become
> A lady like me; with a love, even such,
> So, and no other, *as yourself commanded*:
> Which, not to have done, I think had been in me
> Both disobedience and ingratitude
> To you, and toward your friend, whose love had spoke,
> Even since it could speak, from an infant, freely,
> That it was yours.
> (III, ii, 61–71; italics mine)

Hermione's affection for Polixenes is genuine, she says, and it originates in her husband; Leontes commanded that she emulate his admirable friendship for his childhood companion and she willingly obeyed.

She read this command less in what he said directly to her than in the kind of pressure exemplified by his behavior after Polixenes' announcement of his departure, when he felt personally betrayed by what he interpreted as her indifference.

Hermione confirms that her husband has truly been her mimetic model in her relationship with Polixenes. Leontes has discovered something real but he misinterprets this reality which is perfectly innocent, not at all what he imagines.

The hyper-mimetic Leontes puts his wife in a classical *double bind*. Whatever she does, she can only do wrong in his eyes: if she remains prudently aloof, she seems insensitive; if she displays her sympathy for Polixenes, she is accused of adultery.

Leontes is the supreme expert on mimetic desire; he sees himself as the wrong kind of mimetic model not only to Hermione and Polixenes but to Camillo. His psychology is going awry but for more complex and subtle reasons than is generally perceived. He cannot be dismissed as a senseless madman.

*   *   *

Leontes' famous soliloquy on *affection* is often presented as one of the most obscure, perhaps the most obscure text in all of Shakespeare. In the light of what we just found, this obscurity vanishes:

> Affection! thy intention stabs at the centre.
> Thou dost make possible things not so held,
> Communicat'st with dreams (how can this be?)
> With what's unreal thou co-active art,
> And fellow'st nothing. Then, 'tis very credent
> Thou may co-join with something, and thou dost
> (And that beyond commission), and I find it
> (And that to the infection of my brains
> And hard'ning of my brows).
>   (I, ii, 138–146)

It is just as natural for Leontes to reflect on our ability to penetrate the true feelings of fellow human beings as it is to the jealous narrator in Marcel Proust's *Remembrance of Things Past*. His statement looks somewhat chaotic but it is supposed to reflect a chaotic state of mind and a somewhat chaotic form makes dramatic sense. Shakespeare's own mimetic views are faithfully reproduced in this text and everything Leontes says is perfectly coherent from their standpoint.

Some commentators think that the word *affection* refers to Leontes and his jealousy, others that it means the presumed desire of Hermione for Polixenes and vice versa. From Leontes' perspective, these three desires, being copied on each other, are the same. Instead of choosing between the two interpretations, as if they were incompatible, we must combine them. "Affection" is inseparable from "infection" and it means mimetic desire in all its modalities.

To Shakespeare it goes without saying that we not only misunderstand but understand other people by *projecting* our own sentiments upon them. In *Twelfth Night*, for instance, Orsino discusses Olivia's desire on the sole basis of his own. In our text, too, the projective nature of all attempts to grasp other desires is taken for granted.

If desire *fellows nothing*, if it does not reproduce itself mimetically, the subjective image that it projects has no objective counterpart; we think that we understand something outside ourselves when, in reality, we grasp nothing but phantoms.

Either desire produces no real knowledge because it has no mimetic off-spring or it produces the desired knowledge because it has already produced the object of that knowledge.

Not all projections are deceptive, therefore; if they all were, there would be no knowledge at all of other people's desires. Shakespeare does not acknowledge our convenient distinction between, on the one hand, a projective and "subjective" knowledge which would always be false and, on the other hand, an "objective" knowledge which could be "scientific" and true. The idea of a non-subjective *unconscious* that can be explored methodically enables Freud to reintroduce objective knowledge by the back door. The same is true with Lacan's mythical distinction between what he calls the "symbolique" and the "imaginaire." For Shakespeare, all knowledge of desire is projective.

We have at least four different words or metaphors in this text for the mimetic knowledge of mimetic desire. One is the image of fatherhood; another is the idea of communication; a third is the theme of a desire that may or may not *co-join* with another, a desire that is separate and yet intimately related to the first, since begotten by it, or its begetter. All these formulas base the true knowledge of desire in the effective participation of the knower in what is known. Our text is an extraordinary essay on the very subject of the present book, *thou co-active art!*, mimetic desire and the knowledge thereof.

If a co-production of desires has already occurred, Leontes' partners already love one another as intensely as Leontes loves them and it is "beyond commission": his cuckoldry, the *hard'ning of his brows*, coincides with *the infection of his brain*, with his forever increasing mimetic obsession.

Leontes correctly assumes that he has fathered Hermione's feelings for Polixenes. Between the two possibilities that he outlines, he makes the right choice. As soon as he realizes, however, that success had crowned his efforts and that the sympathy truly exists that he spent so much time nurturing between Hermione and Polixenes, his self-distrust makes him feel excluded from this relationship; he transforms it into some kind of alliance against him, an adulterous complicity.

Like many modern interpreters, Leontes goes wrong by "excès de soup-çon. His wife's affection for Polixenes is his own child but he misunderstands it. His insecurity always goes straight to the worst possible interpretation from his own standpoint and his dreadful error is inseparable from his shrewd mimetic insight. Far from helping him in his hour of need, his perspicacity precipitates his downfall.

Such is the fate of many a theorist! To know if imitation has occurred is difficult enough but, even if we guess right on this point, we may still go wrong regarding the kind of imitation that we have discovered.

* * *

Hermione owed her love for Polixenes to a mediation that remains pure, innocent, and respectful of the rights and duties of all parties involved, even though no barrier separates the two characters. At the instant when Leontes' jealousy is born, Polixenes and Hermione treat each other as familiarly as if they were brother and sister. Their loss of inhibition greatly contributes to the jealousy of Leontes.

The power that arrests the infernal consequences of unobstructed mimesis is first of all Hermione herself, her good sense, her innate nobility of spirit, the wise use she makes of her freedom. There is not an ounce of *bovarysme* in her and she is more genuinely admirable than the women generally regarded as such in Shakespeare, the Juliets and the Desdemonas who benefit in our eyes from a mimetic aura rooted in their mimetic propensities. Shakespeare is so great that we tend to read and misread his imaginary creations as we all read and misread the human beings around us.

Judging from what happens in the second half of the play, Polixenes is less exceptional a human being than Hermione but it does not matter. A man does not have to be a moral giant, necessarily, to abstain from lusting after the wife of his best friend. He may have a thousand other things on his mind about which the author does not have to inform us. We must not forget, besides, that Hermione has never done anything to lead Polixenes into temptation. This is what her husband foolishly resented a little earlier; he found her insufferably reserved with his dear friend.

Leontes is not uniformly systematic in his thinking; he does not mistake the mimetic principle for the causal law that it is not. He makes allowance for desires that "fellow nothing." He has been dreaming of the very *innocent* love that now exists between Polixenes and Hermione. And yet, when confronted with the proof of its existence, he feels overwhelmed with jealousy.

The more remote the chance that, somewhere in the real world, some real innocence exists, the more monstrous it is to mistake it for its opposite and try to crush it. Leontes not only does not recognize the true nature of those closest to him but, being the main beneficiary of the good that he misunderstands, he cannot destroy it without destroying himself. The stupidity of this enormous intelligence is even more abysmal than its guilt.

Leontes resembles the way in which Shakespeare himself long applied the mimetic law in his own theater, creating plays from which innocence was practically banished. Innocence was especially impossible in the case of triangles involving childhood friends.

As late as *Coriolanus*, Shakespeare alluded to the mimetic ambivalence of close friends as if it were a law of nature. If we re-read the words of Aufidius on the subject, we may find it easier to apprehend Leontes' state of mind:

> Friends now fast sworn,
> Whose double bosoms seems to wear one heart,
> Whose heart, whose bed, whose meal and exercise
> Are still together, who twin, as 'twere, in love
> Unseparable, shall within this hour
> On a dissension of a doit, break out
> To bitterest enmity. . . .
>   (IV, iii, 12–18)

* * *

Among the plays of unfounded jealousy, *The Winter's Tale* is not unusual solely for its innocent childhood friend and its innocent wife. Something else makes it exceptional in its category, and it is the lack of a villain. In order to assess the significance of this feature, let us first recall the dramatic function of Don John in *Much Ado About Nothing* and of Iago in *Othello*.

When the two heroes of these plays are interpreted in mimetic terms, it becomes clear that their jealousy operates just like the jealousy of Leontes; it is just as self-induced and just as self-explanatory. From the standpoint of the "deeper plays," Don John and Iago are superfluous. Only if we remain blind to the mimetic genesis of the two dramas, shall we need the villains to account for the heroes' jealousy.

If, for some reason, the real explanation escapes us, the villains will provide a slightly contrived but serviceable replacement. They are sacrificial instruments in the strict sense since their function depends squarely on scapegoating. The villainy of the villains diverts toward itself the indignation that Claudio and Othello would certainly arouse if no external "motivation" were provided for their cruel and criminal behavior.

Without the villains, the spectators could not identify at all with the heroes. Don John and Iago are the two pillars upon which the "superficial" versions of their two respective plays are erected. The difference between a "superficial play" and a "deeper play," I recall, is that the mimetic interaction visible in the latter is invisible in the former.

In *Much Ado About Nothing* and in *Othello*, the sacrificial structure generated by the scapegoating of the villain is similar to the one generated by the scapegoating of Shylock in *The Merchant of Venice*. As soon as we begin to understand the victimage mechanism, the sacrificial interpretation weakens and the mimetic one threatens. We can see this clearly if we compare the critical reception of *Much Ado About Nothing* to that of *Othello*. Even though Claudio is the less criminal of the two heroes, more puzzled eyebrows have been raised in his direction than in the direction of Othello, and the only possible reason is that Don John is a much thinner villain than the sinister Iago, much less satisfying as a sacrificial offering.

The criticism often addressed to *The Winter's Tale* makes the dramatic function of Shakespeare's villains even more obvious. The traditional critics have always found Leontes simultaneously disturbing and unintelligible. Complaining that his jealousy is "insufficiently motivated," they find him unsatisfactory as a protagonist of "serious drama." In reality, he is an Othello without his Iago, a Claudio without his Don John, the full revelation of a truth still partly veiled in the previous plays.

Leontes should be the greatest symbol of jealousy in the theater of Shakespeare but we can well understand why Othello was selected instead. He is more colorful in every way, of course, but the main reason lies elsewhere. Jealousy is a sentiment in which we all share to some extent and it must be mitigated by sacrifice. The image projected by Leontes is too stark for universal consumption.

The standard form of drama—in contradistinction with tragedy—is the *hero* versus *villain* dichotomy; popular success demands that this scheme be forever repeated. The differentiation it requires must be founded on some villainous culprit whose punishment the spectators anticipate with relish. This sacrificial scapegoat must polarize their hostilities in such a way as to deflect them from the hero whose identical *double* he really is. To interact with the hero on equal terms, the villain must be sufficiently like him and yet, to qualify as a villain, he must be strikingly different. These contradictory requirements are characteristic of all sacrificial victims everywhere, beginning with ritual immolation.

In *The Winter's Tale*, Shakespeare throws all precautions to the wind and removes the props from under the *superficial play*. The whole horrendous truth is unmasked and the author makes it even more horrendous by having Leontes destroy his childhood friendship and his entire family as well as the woman he loves. Compared to his two forerunners, he looks like a darker version of something already quite dark. He is the most intelligent, the most depressive, the most destructive of all Shakespearean hypermimetic characters.

It must not be a mere coincidence if the suppression of the villain occurs in the very same play that radicalizes the evil of mimetic self-poisoning and makes one of the two childhood friends innocent for the first time. This conjunction suggests that Shakespeare is coming to terms with something in his past that wanted to emerge into the light but did not quite succeed.

* * *

Leontes and Polixenes were childhood friends. In his private conversation with Hermione, Polixenes portrays this friendship in idyllic terms:

> We were as twinn'd lambs that did frisk i' th' sun,
> And bleat the one at th' other: what we chang'd
> Was innocence for innocence: we knew not
> The doctrine of ill-doing, nor dream'd
> That any did.
>   (I, ii, 67–71)

Childhood friends are as far from actual sin as any two human beings can be; all they exchange is *innocence for innocence*. And yet, as they grow up, they turn to ravening wolves, either simultaneously or successively; it does not matter. Even in these lambs, especially in them, the potential for evil is enormous and perfectly continuous with the innocence in which it is rooted.

This is the transparent mystery that has always haunted Shakespeare. At the very end of his dramatic career, he resumes a meditation that can already be detected behind the apparent frivolity of *The Two Gentlemen of Verona*:

> *Polixenes*: Had we pursu'd that life,
> And our weak spirits ne'er been higher rear'd
> With stronger blood, we should have answer'd heaven
> Boldly 'not guilty', the imposition clear'd
> Hereditary ours.
>   (71–74)

The meekness of the lambs is often invoked as an argument against the idea of original sin. Assailing the supposed ferocity of this doctrine, indignant philanthropists point to childhood innocence as a spectacular proof of the theologians' perversity. Shakespeare could not disagree more.

If the twinned lambs are the best that human beings can do in the way of innocence, if senseless conflict is always already lurking behind the relationship that comes closest to our idea of perfection, how can the thesis of intrinsically innocent man be defended? In the author's eyes, the lambs are not a refutation of original sin but a striking confirmation.

Rising above the malice and matter of earlier plays, *The Winter's Tale* invites us to confront the spirit of discord in all its horror. This time, the meditation on the childhood friends does not dissolve in the ambivalence of perverse desire; it leads straight to the doctrine of the fall. Hermione is a good listener and she understands the allusion:

> By this we gather
> You have tripped since.
> (75–76)

And Polixenes answers:

> O my most sacred lady,
> Temptations have since then been born to's: for
> In those unfledg'd days was my wife a girl;
> Your precious self had then not cross'd the eyes
> Of my young play-fellow.
> (76–80)

Until these last lines, Polixenes was doing quite well but now he is going astray: it cannot be fair to blame the quarrel of the mimetic twins on woman, simply because she happens to be in the middle. Whenever the mimetic *doubles* are seeking some temporary reconciliation, they achieve it at her expense. She is their common scapegoat; she is not the real explanation.

We would be poor readers, at this point, if we believed that Polixenes is still speaking for Shakespeare. The fact that an opinion appears in a writer's work, and that it was popular when he was alive, does not necessarily mean that he approved of it. If we want to know what Shakespeare really thought, we must wait for Hermione's reply to Polixenes:

> Grace to boot!
> Of this make no conclusion, lest you say
> Your queen and I are devils.
> (I, ii, 75–82)

The word *devil*, diabolos, signifies not some inert obstacle but the stumbling block of the law and the prophets, the *skandalon* of the gospels, the obstacle that fascinates us more and more as we keep painfully colliding with it, the crisscrossing of rivalrous desires. The character who illustrates this phenomenon in our play is obviously Leontes and, later on, Polixenes; it cannot be Hermione.

Hermione is not speaking against the biblical idea of the fall, but against an interpretation that badly distorts the text of Genesis; it prevents its mimetic significance from emerging. Eve is first to sin, no doubt, but her chronological anteriority does not make her a real origin. Just as she listens to the serpent, Adam listens to Eve. She is to him what the serpent is to her, a mimetic mediator. The two human beings become a continuation of the serpent and their respective place on its coils does not make either one more guilty than the other, or less. Eve's desire is in no way different from Adam's, neither more nor less mimetic.

In his answer to God's query, Adam blames everything on Eve; he has been repeating this accusation ever since, in the teeth of a biblical text that, far from condoning his cowardly avoidance of responsibility obviously regards it as a continuation and aggravation of the original sin. There is no biblical reason for singling out Eve as the main culprit.

Only from the narrowest perspective—the forever non-mimetic perspective of Adam—can the chronological priority of Eve be turned into a sacrificial mitigation of Adam's sin. From the beginning, Adam has tried to transform a minor point into the total message of the story. He does this in order to elude the truth of his desire. What we inherited from him is both the desire and the appetite for scapegoating that goes with it.

It is typical of the current intellectual situation; instead of going back to the biblical source and of reading it with an eye free from prejudice, many contemporary feminists still docilely accept Adam's interpretation of the fall and blame the book of Genesis for the gender discrimination that it really stigmatizes. The anti-feminist bias is so entrenched that it triumphs with the feminists themselves. Fortunately, a few highly perceptive readers, whose brilliant insight I am now following, have discovered in the text of Genesis the priceless model of mimetic interpretation that it really is.[1]

* * *

The debate of Polixenes and Hermione is not an attack against original sin, I repeat, but an implicit refutation of the reading that empties it of its real content and turns it into another scapegoat recipe at the expense of woman. This distortion paradoxically and shamefully exemplifies the way in which biblical ideas are turned into their own opposites. The real idea of original sin is that human beings are all equally guilty, guilty of scapegoating, of course. Even though Shakespeare does not explicitly say so, the "twinned lambs" and their sinister transformation inevitably suggest themselves as a better archetype for original sin than the victimization of Eve.

After rejecting Polixenes' view, Hermione does not propose her own view of original sin but she does not have to. Polixenes' own emphasis on the "twinned lambs" does it for her, and so does the drama as a whole, of course. Whenever Shakespeare thinks of original sin, he has his childhood friends and brothers in mind, I feel. In *Hamlet*, his biblical reference is Cain and Abel: Claudius rightly feels that his own sin is the sin par excellence, *the primal eldest curse, a brother's murther*. *The Winter's Tale* suggests the same definition. It is not fortuitous that, in Genesis, Cain and Abel immediately follow Adam and Eve. The two stories define the whole mimetic process in a nutshell.

The focusing on original sin and the refusal of malice and matter are two aspects of the same vision. But before sin can be acknowledged as this original sin portrayed in Genesis, it must be cleansed of the distortion against which Hermione rightly protests, at the very instant when she becomes its victim. Hermione is no devil but she is always treated like one, first in the words of Polixenes, and then in the deeds of Leontes. The debate of Polixenes and Hermione is a religious and philosophical condensation of *The Winter's Tale* as a whole, its spiritual *mise-en-abime*.

Polixenes' unfair singling out of woman is prophetic not only of Leontes' injustice against Hermione but of his own injustice against Perdita in the second half of the play. Leontes and Polixenes are very much alike; they deserve one another more than they realize.

II

V, i, could be entitled: "The last temptation of Leontes." Sixteen years after the tragedy of the first three acts, Polixenes' son, Florizel, arrives in Sicilia in the company of Leontes' long-lost daughter Perdita, whose identity is unknown. The couple is fleeing the rage of a royal father who does not want his son to marry the humble shepherdess that Perdita seems to be. During their first meeting with the king, these young people claim that Polixenes himself sent them as ambassadors to his old friend, but the truth is suddenly revealed and Florizel begs Leontes to be his go-between with his father:

> Step forth as mine advocate. At your request
> My father will grant precious things as trifles.
>   (V, i, 221–22)

Leontes' reply shows that he is greatly attracted to Perdita:

> Would he do so, I'ld beg your precious mistress,
> Which he counts as a trifle.
>   (223–224)

The ever watchful Paulina fiercely reminds the old king of his dead wife:

> Sir, my liege,
> Your eye hath too much youth in't. Not a month
> 'Fore your queen died, she was more worth such gazes
> Than what you look on now.
> *Leontes*: I thought of her,
> Even in these looks I made.
>   (224–228)

Leontes is not lying; far from forgetting Hermione, he remembers her too vividly. Perdita looks so much like her mother and Florizel so much like his father that the entire past seems resurrected.

The same insolent happiness radiates from Florizel and Perdita as from Polixenes and Hermione sixteen years earlier, when they held hands in front of Leontes, and Leontes, once again, feels the pangs of jealousy; once again he feels excluded from paradise. These lovers ask for a protector but, in Leontes' eyes, they do not need any; they seem divinely invulnerable and self-sufficient.

The gleam that Paulina sees in Leontes' eyes reflects Florizel's desire for Perdita, Perdita's desire for Florizel. Once again, Leontes is threatened by mimetic contagion.

This scene resurrects a past that never was, the distorted past of Leontes' jealousy. This time, the presumed lovers truly desire each other; they have truly asked Leontes to be their go-between. This true repetition of a false original gives a deceptive ring of authenticity to the old obsession. We can well understand why, once again, Leontes is tempted to appropriate this happiness or, if he cannot, destroy it.

Unless we perceive this uncanny repetition of Leontes' most dreadful experience, we fail to understand why he comes so close to stumbling a second time; we do not feel the sympathy that, for the first time, he deserves. The main point of the episode is not his temptation but his final victory which contrasts with his earlier defeat. The scene is not supposed to undermine but to strengthen the credibility of Leontes' repentance.

* * *

At the end of this brief episode, Leontes once again addresses Florizel:

> But your petition
> Is yet unanswer'd. I will to your father.

Your honor not o'erthrown by your desires,
I am friend to them and you.
(228–231; italics mine)

Leontes' personal crisis is over and a happy end is in sight for the two lovers.
All this is too obvious, it seems, to require further comment.

And yet the last line is curiously worded. Instead of saying, "I am your
friend," Leontes first says: "I am friend to them," meaning "your desires."
Should we assume that the two expressions are equivalent and that the final
"and you" is superfluous? Everything we learned in this book suggests that the
arrangement of the words "friends," "desire" and "you" is a calculated allusion
to the mimetic ambivalence of the situation.

If two desires are each other's friends, they will covet the same object,
the same Perdita, and the men whose desires they are will not end up as
friends but as enemies. The friendship of men means harmony and peace, the
friendship of their desires means jealousy and war. Until the final "and you,"
the words of Leontes harbor the dark possibility of a new tragedy.

Shakespeare is once again playing with the desire that, in *A Midsummer
Night's Dream*, "stood upon the choice of friends." Once again, the words
"friend" and "friendship" suggest the insidious nature of mimetic rivalry, its
tendency to creep up on us when our intentions are most pure. We may hon-
estly believe that the interest of a friend still governs our actions when, in fact,
for the sake of this friend's desire, the friendship is already betrayed.

The last line sums up the temporality of Leontes' experience. After:
"I am friend to them," meaning your desires, the actor who plays Leontes
should pause briefly for an almost imperceptible sigh of regret, and then, his
"and you" should sound like the words of a man suddenly relieved of an invisible burden. This victory over temptation should be discreet, to be sure, but
not so discreet as to remain invisible.

In the following scene (V, ii), we learn that Paulina had invited Leontes
and his guests, Polixenes, Camillo, Florizel and Perdita, to unveil with her a
wonderfully true-to-life statue of their late wife, mother and friend. The statue
is Hermione herself who has been living for sixteen years at Paulina's house.

In the final scene (V, iii), Leontes sees the statue and is taken aback by
its marvelous resemblance to his wife. The loving husband is deeply moved,
but there is a second man in him, a Renaissance connoisseur who still wants
to be heard. Meticulously inspecting the strange object offered to his curios-
ity, he comes up with a remarkable finding:

But yet Paulina
Hermione was not so much wrinkled, nothing

So aged as this seems.
   (V, iii, 26–29)

According to Paulina, the sculptor wanted to portray Hermione *as she liv'd now*. So great was his devotion to the true-to-life that he was true even to the life that was not. A less complicated Leontes might have guessed, at this point, that the good lady is pulling his leg; our man suspects nothing. Being convinced that, sixteen years before, his blind rage destroyed his wife, he understandably resists the message of his senses. His stubbornness is too great, however, not to require an additional explanation. Discreetly, Shakespeare points to aesthetic snobbery.

In the chic world of Sicilia, a smart gentleman must never confuse even the most perfect copy with the copied original. According to some Greek writer, some Greek birds were so completely fooled by the grapes on some Greek painting—the painter was a superchampion of the true-to-life—that they tried to eat them. Who wants to resemble these birds?

"Modern artists have become so good," Leontes says to himself, "that they can fool us all; I will not be fooled; I will not believe that this statue is my wife; I will stick to the stone that my eyes insist it cannot be." In the world of Leontes, already, the greatest shame is *to be taken in by representation*. With each generation this shame takes a slightly different form but it is still with us.

Contemporary intellectuals keep chiding their fellow men for their assuredly deplorable but also rather touching tendency to confuse signs with the objects for which they stand. What about the reverse illusion? We have done so well that we made it unthinkable. A mere sign would turn into real being? Even if we saw this miracle with our own eyes, we would find it so scandalous that we would not believe it. Leontes is very much like us. He is so much on guard against one type of illusion that he proves defenseless against the opposite type. For the innocent wiles of Paulina and Hermione, he is the ideal dupe.

Shakespeare is gently deriding the Western gullibility par excellence, the obsession with gullibility. When in doubt, experts always choose disbelief. This is what makes them experts. Like everybody else, the poor Leontes wants to be an expert and, in matters aesthetic as well as erotic, he seeks safety in a denial of his own perception. This is a new variation of a mimetic story that Shakespeare told many times: *love by hearsay, love by another's eye*. The statue as statue is the equivalent of the *hard-hearted adamant* towards which all midsummer night lovers instinctively gravitate. Between pure joy and a stone, we play it safe and choose the stone.

We should not think ill of Leontes because of this. The depth of his repentance is not in question. Hermione comes first in his mind:

O, thus she stood,
Even with such life of majesty, warm life,
As now it coldly stands, when first I woo'd,
I am asham'd; does not the stone rebuke me
For being more stone than it?
    (34–38)

Leontes has changed, and so suddenly that the minor aspects of his personality have remained the same; he needs more time to adjust. His aesthetic fashionability clings to him like wet clothes to the back of a man who just saved someone from drowning, someone who happens to be himself; he is too excited to think of changing shirts.

If this *jeu de scène* involves nothing essential, why have it at all? Symbolically, its importance is enormous. Leontes' hesitation recapitulates his former mimetic predicament with Hermione. The conclusion repeats the whole drama in a nutshell; it reactualizes Leontes' "tragic flaw" in a minor key, so that we can see his old sinfulness vanish once and for all before our eyes.

At first, we, in the audience, are just as ignorant as the hero; we think that Hermione is dead. When first unveiled, the "statue" should seem genuinely sculptural and lifeless. We discover the truth slowly but less slowly than Leontes.

When the wrinkles are first mentioned, the lighting should improve. Recognizing the actress who plays Hermione, we grasp the whole truth, but Leontes does not. Having briefly shared in his error, we can understand it. For the first time, we fully sympathize with the hero. . . .

* * *

V, i and V, iii, stand in sharp contrast to each other. The author visibly intended to have a "false" resurrection of Hermione followed by a "true" one. The juxtaposition of the two is obviously intentional and it confirms the pertinence of the word *resurrection.*

Neither incident is really a resurrection, of course; they both are the unexpected reappearance of a long lost woman in the life of Leontes, first his daughter and then his wife. In the first scene, when Leontes sees Perdita, he is so powerfully reminded of his wife that she seems *resurrected*; this illusion is persuasive at first but it vanishes as quickly as it appeared, as soon as the temptation that it triggers is vanquished.

In this mirage of mimetic desire, the resurrected Hermione appears as youthful as she was when Leontes last saw her, as if some magical eternity had nullified the sixteen years in-between.

The second scene reverses the false impressions of the first and Hermione's body bears the stigma of historical time. That is the reason for her wrinkles. The second resurrection is as *true* as the first was false. It is Leontes' reward for purging his bad desire. This spiritual truth is also the literal truth. Greatly afraid at first by her master's last temptation, then completely reassured, the wise Paulina has decided that Hermione could safely rejoin her husband.

The word *resurrection* is certainly appropriate, even unavoidable from the only perspective that counts in this scene, the perspective of Leontes. I see no shame in using it.

Hermione's wrinkles should not be a source of misunderstanding. It is understandable that Leontes would find them puzzling *on a statue*. We should not think that, as soon as the curtain goes down, he will dream of a face lift for his wife, or perhaps of a quick divorce for himself. Nowadays, of course, he might have to. He is a successful man, after all, and he should be surrounded with nothing but impeccable objects. He should make sure, above all, that his sex objects arouse the *envy* of other men.

The *bawd and cuckold* imperative has reached such cost. . . . mimetic proportions in our "complicated" modern world—this is what the media always call it—that we mistake it for an ethical principle, our only indestructible one. Leontes' Renaissance world was less "complicated" to start with, I presume, and his conversion has further "simplified" it.

* * *

The statue scene is a unique reversal of a relationship between truth and illusion, being and non-being, that had always prevailed in Shakespeare before *The Winter's Tale*. In all comedies and tragedies, we always found the main thrust to be away from immediacy, toward more and more mimesis, more metaphysical illusion. Things that first passed for genuine were shown to be fictional; representations supposedly true turned out to be false; those false from the start vanished entirely. Sharp distinctions got blurred; clarity gave way to confusion. Harmonious shapes contaminated each other and became monstrous. Famous men disappeared and reappeared as phantoms. Form disintegrated; differences collapsed; hard objects liquefied, making "a sop of all this solid globe." Symbols unraveled; nothingness triumphed.

One could object that, in many previous plays, the ending already suggested a return to reality. This is true but, in all previous conclusions, the alleged reversal was only a fiction of the *superficial play*, based on some sacrificial trickery, discreetly but effectively undermined by the *deeper play*. Degree itself stands exposed as the fruit of collective violence and is discredited.

The ending of *The Winter's Tale* is something else entirely. The triumph of being is genuine, this time, no longer rooted in sacrificial death. What could be the cause of this revolution? Earlier, we found that many obsessive themes of Shakespeare reappear in this play but always with a difference. Leontes' mimetic psychology is as subtle and profound as Shakespeare's own and yet, when put to the test, it fails miserably. Is the paranoid insight stigmatized in this play the author's condemnation of his own implacable psychology? Are the women persecuted in all the romances mere figments of his imagination or are they real women? For the first time, his meditation on the mimetic *doubles* leads the author to the notion of original sin. Does all this reflect a demystification of the demystificatory stance, a self-critical, even a penitential mood?

The conversion/resurrection of Leontes greatly bolsters this hypothesis. In the light of our previous discussion, it can hardly be a gratuitous fabrication; it must be rooted in the many aspects of this play and of previous plays that seem to call for it.

How did Shakespeare shift from the brilliant but desperate cynicism of a *Troilus and Cressida* to the attitude suggested by the second half of *The Winter's Tale*? His conversion mood does not look like an aesthetic caprice to me. It takes hold gradually and its first expression, Posthumus, sounds curiously awkward for such a powerful and experienced writer as Shakespeare. Posthumus, nevertheless, clearly prefigures the masterful handling of Leontes' repentance.

If we assume that the creator put a great deal of himself in these heroes, the specific difference of all themes in *The Winter's Tale* makes perfect sense, including Acts III and IV which we did not examine at all. As Shakespeare became more severe with himself, his tolerance of others increased and his portrayal of innocence acquired the power that it lacks in the first two romances. I see *The Winter's Tale* and its conclusion as the indirect account of a creative experience based on the author's deepening awareness that his past ferocity with sufferers of mimetic desire was still fueled by the virulence of the disease in himself.

I see *The Winter's Tale* as the successful accomplishment of a purpose that long remained unconscious and that can be traced back not only to the first two romances, but to the Cordelia of *King Lear*, more obscurely to the horror of *Othello*, to the sacrificial nausea of *Hamlet*, even to the plays most colored by nihilism, the fierce *Troilus and Cressida*, for instance, where it can be read only in the frenzy of its own negation, in the systematic eradication of anything even remotely conceivable as *redemptive*.

* * *

The self-involvement of a writer in his work is often regarded as something beyond the reach of the critic and now the idea is less popular than ever; it collides with the fashionable conception of literature as "verbal play." Even *mimesis* is enlisted in this battle, by the very same people who, in principle, deny all relevance to it. Writers are such *mimes*, we are told, that they can feign a thousand states of mind which they never experience themselves. This is true, no doubt, but it is not the whole truth and partial truths are misleading. What a genuine writer truly desires to represent is his own state of mind.

The arguments against the writer's involvement in his work never impressed me very much and, in the case of *The Winter's Tale*, they impress me less than ever. They remind me too much of Leontes in front of his statue. We do not want to be *taken in by representation*. Moved by the fear of appearing naive, contemporary critics stick to the illusion of an illusion; their false idea of art blinds them to the real Hermione behind the false statue.

The spiritual experience I read behind *The Winter's Tale* is deduced from the texts; it is not an "autobiographical" hypothesis, it is not an "opinion" or "belief" that I would gratuitously attribute to a man named William Shakespeare.

A writer's greatness as a mimetic revealer inevitably entails, at some point in his career, a concrete coming to terms with the truth of the *doubles*, and this experience can only occur at his own expense, at a severe cost to his mimetic ego. To accede to the mimetic awareness that structures his works, he must discover his identity with the targets of his own satire; he must accept the collapse of whatever mythical *difference* mattered most in his personal system of self-justification. Not theoretically but in his own flesh, he must verify the literal truth of Paul's words to the Romans (2.1):

> Therefore thou art inexcusable, O man, whosoever thou art that judgest: for wherein thou judgest another, thou condemnest thyself; for thou that judgest does the same things.

All writing that reenacts the mimetic truth of human relations necessarily originates in a spiritual experience that can write itself either directly as repentance, as it does in *The Winter's Tale*, or, metaphorically, as death, illness, or some other kind of personal catastrophe, upon which a resurrection symbolism is grafted.

Mimetic circularity is not a question of "feeling," of ideology, of religious belief; it is the intractable structure of human conflict explicitly acknowledged only in Jewish and Christian Scripture. All great writers implicitly acknowledge this truth but not all do so explicitly. Ignorance, residual prejudice and other factors are in the way.

It does not really matter; the experience itself always assumes the same characteristic form which is the form of sacrifice, the "death and resurrection" pattern, but in a paradoxical inversion, since the substance is non-sacrificial. Instead of some kind of scapegoat transference, we have the very reverse, a return of the subject upon himself, genuine self-criticism.

In my work on the European novel I found that, in all major novelists, there exists one key work, sometimes two, or even more, whose conclusions, although far from uniform, all belong to the same easily recognizable group because they all reproduce the death and resurrection pattern.

This pattern is banal and it may signify very little but it may also refer to the experience I have just defined, so fundamental to the greatness of great works and so powerful that the creators are irresistibly led to allude to it, generally at the place in the work which is best suited to the purpose, the conclusion. In *Deceit, Desire and the Novel*, I named these significant conclusions "conversions romanesques," a misleading label, I am afraid, since this phenomenon transcends all literary distinctions, including distinctions of genre.

I see the conclusion of *The Winter's Tale* as the first example of such a *creative conversion* in Shakespeare, and an exceptional one, not only for its beauty and its late date in the chronology of its creator, but for the extraordinary typicality of its overall structure, secured through means that seem entirely original with Shakespeare.

Whereas in most novels, the *resurrection* aspect is reduced to a few words, Shakespeare expands this meagre symbolism to the majestic dimensions of the statue scene. The reverse is true of *death*, the other pole of this dual structure. Whereas death reigns supreme at the end of most novels, in our conclusion, it is reduced to an absolute minimum, the slightly prolonged but still short-lived illusion that Hermione exists only as a piece of stone.

If these conclusions really mean what I think they do, death in them, being defeated by resurrection, should appear only as a briefly dominant, and then quickly discredited idea, a fast vanishing background. This seems impossible to achieve without fantastic tricks that would ruin the whole enterprise from the start and yet Shakespeare achieved it with the greatest of ease in *The Winter's Tale*. If he had deliberately set out to illustrate the process of non-sacrificial death and resurrection, he could not have gone about it more effectively than he did in this conclusion.

* * *

Even though this conclusion has no overtly religious content, its similarity with certain resurrection scenes in the Christian gospels is too remarkable to be fortuitous.

Whenever Jesus appears after his Resurrection, his disciples cannot recognize him immediately. Mary Magdalen mistakes him for a gardener; the

Emmaus disciples see him as an ordinary traveler. Thomas' doubts are a variation on the same theme. What is the meaning of this delayed recognition?

The reason lies not with Jesus but with the disciples who are never "converted enough." Their imperfection is structurally specific in the sense of always revolving around some kind of obstacle perceived as an external reality, even though it originates in the individuals themselves. This obstacle accompanies the would-be convert for a while, as a minor but stubborn impediment on his road to a higher faith and then, with the attainment of that faith, it disappears without a trace. Conversion and resurrection are thus closely interrelated, and this is especially true in Mark, whose original ending is extremely short.

Two days after the crucifixion, the holy women want to give Jesus a proper burial. As they proceed toward the tomb on Easter morning, they worry about the large stone that shuts the entrance, too heavy for them to push aside. When they arrive, the stone has been removed and the tomb is empty (16.1–4).

In *The Winter's Tale*, the statue plays a role similar to this stone. It is the obstacle to the recognition of Hermione. Even as Leontes feels the warmth of her hands, he still cannot believe that she is alive.

The stone and the statue are symbolic concretions of the mimetic stumbling block. In spite of its unreality, this *skandalon* is enormously constraining; it stems from the intersubjective—interdividual—collaboration of mimetic rivalry and it structures not our individual psyches only but the entire human world; it imprisons us all in its circular pattern. The violence that it generates is the real origin of the false forms of transcendence that severely limit our vision. As we already know, this principle of idolatry makes sacrifices indispensable because it cuts us off not only from God but from one another.

The women on their way to the tomb are as prepared to see their Lord as human beings can ever be, but our human best is still not enough on such occasions; there is always some *skandalon* left in our eyes to perpetuate our blindness. This is what the delayed recognition signifies, both in the gospels and in *The Winter's Tale*.

For the statue scene to be fully effective, the stone to which Hermione seems reduced must signify not only her physical death in the eyes of Leontes but, more importantly still, his own spiritual death. Shakespeare made all this completely clear by having Leontes himself, at the end of our last quote, point to the twofold significance of this symbolism:

> Does not the stone rebuke me
> For being more stone than it?

Already in *Othello*, in very much the same context, stone is an image of spiritual death. When the Moor is about to kill Desdemona and her protestations of innocence cause him to doubt her guilt for the first time, he feels his heart turn to stone:

O, perjur'd woman, thou dost stone my heart,
And mak'st me call what I intend to do
A murther which I thought a sacrifice.
    (*Othello*, V, ii, 63–65)

This is how Leontes has been feeling ever since he discovered the innocence of his wife, thinking he had killed her. With one line only, Shakespeare transforms Othello's confession of guilt into a revelation of sacrifice. Man is this strange animal who insists on calling his murders sacrifice, as if he were obeying the command of some god.

The revelation of sacrifice as murder is not Othello's truth only but the truth of *Julius Caesar*, the truth of all tragedy, the ultimate truth of sacrificial culture, the truth that informs *The Winter's Tale* even more fully than any previous play, the greatest truth uncovered by Shakespeare, and it also comes from the gospels.

The fact that Othello not only understands this truth but applies it to himself, makes him another forerunner of Leontes. What makes our hearts turn to stone is the discovery that, in one sense or another, we are all butchers pretending to be sacrificers. When we understand this, the *skandalon* that we had always managed to discharge upon some scapegoat, becomes our own responsibility, a stone as unbearably heavy upon our hearts as Jesus himself upon the saint's shoulders in the Christopher legend.

One thing alone can put an end to this infernal ordeal, the certainty of being forgiven. This is what Leontes is granted when he finally sees that Hermione is being returned to him alive. This is the first such miracle in Shakespeare; it was still spectacularly impossible at the end in *King Lear* and now it comes to pass for the first time. As the statue turns from stone to flesh, so does the heart of Leontes.

The model for this conclusion can only be the gospel itself, interpreted as this dissolving of the *skandalon* that I have just evoked. Shakespeare must have recognized in the gospels the true revelation not only of God but of man, of what his mimetic imprisonment makes of man.

His genius, and more than his genius enabled Shakespeare to recapture in this conclusion something that belongs exclusively to the gospels, the non-magical and yet non-naturalistic quality of their resurrection. The more we examine the statue scene, the more we are reminded of what that resurrection is supposed to be, a resurrection *of the flesh*, in contradistinction to the vaporous world of spirits conjured up by mimetic idolatry. The delayed recognition of Jesus has nothing to do with a lesser visibility of his resurrected body, due to the lesser reality of the shadowy after-life to which he now would belong. The opposite is true. This resurrection is too real for a perception dimmed by the false transfigurations of mimetic idolatry.

III

Among the many masterpieces of Shakespeare, *The Winter's Tale* deserves a special place, I believe: it is the most moving. Before this play, signs of humility and compassion were not absent from this theater, but they were few, seemingly justifying the presentation of the writer himself as a faceless man, a mere cipher, a non-person, nobody, no one, *nadie*. This is what Jorge Luis Borges did with Shakespeare in his half-whimsical, half-serious interpretation of *El Hacedor*. Using the word *nadie* as his leitmotif, Borges really suggests that the writer bought his genius at the price of his own individual soul.

This Faustian pact with a devil named *mimesis* is a brilliant idea, no doubt, but there is not the slightest evidence behind it, except, of course, for the prodigious genius of Shakespeare, for his almost infinite power of mimetic impersonation, which proves strictly nothing regarding his own personality. Behind Borges' thesis, I read a subtle version of the same fear that we already encountered twice in the last few pages, the Western and modern fear par excellence, the fear of being *taken in by representation*. The faceless Shakespeare is one last mimetic myth, invented by a writer who, not unlike Joyce, understood a great deal about the true role of *mimesis* in literature but always stopped short of the ultimate questioning.

The most eloquent refutation of Borges is *The Winter's Tale* itself, the play in which the humanity of the author shines through as nowhere else, and most brightly, to be sure, at the crucial point where, for the first time in this theater, a transcendental perspective silently opens up.

When competently done, these last moments of the play affect even those with no particular interest in religion in a manner that can only be defined as religious, or bordering on the religious. Irresistibly, the word *resurrection* comes to our lips. Some people are chagrined by this; observing that no actual resurrection occurs and that no religious language is used, they deny a religious dimension to this ending of *The Winter's Tale*.

Is the resurrection effect a fabrication of religious zealots, always trying to inject religion in literature? Even the spectators most receptive to this scene never mistake it for some kind of christianized Pygmalion story. Unless we dogmatically oppose religious effects, for reasons that can hardly be literary, we will acknowledge them just as we would any other kind. To deny this one, on the grounds that there is no explicitly religious discourse behind it, would be tantamount to denying all erotic effects in literature unless accompanied by graphic excerpts from sexological textbooks.

Leontes' triumph over temptation harmonizes with the *jeu de scène* devised by Paulina. If mimetic desire is the devil that discredits and ultimately destroys the real, a genuine renunciation should produce the opposite result. A liberated Leontes should experience *real presence* after all and, indeed, he does . . . with a little delay.

This defeat of mimetic desire is a greater miracle than the violation of some stupid natural law. Once this desire gets a firm grip on someone, it will not relinquish its prey without a battle. The character who dies in Act II and resurrects in Act V is not Hermione but Leontes, and the last scene must be staged from his standpoint.

Reversing T. S. Eliot's language, we shall say that Hermione's apparent resurrection is the subjective correlative of something most objective and real, Leontes' renunciation of his bad desire. The "resurrection effect" occurs when we sense that these two aspects become one in the hero's experience.

NOTE

1. See Raymund Schwager, *Must there be Scapegoats?*, 79; Jean-Michel Oughourlian, *Un mime nommé désir*, 38–44; and Aidan Carl Matthews, "Knowledge of Good and Evil."

WORKS CITED

Matthews, Aidan Carl. "Knowledge of Good and Evil." In *To Honor René Girard*. Saratoga, CA: AnmaLibri, 1986, 17–28.
Oughourlian, Jean-Michel. *Un mime nommé désir*. Paris, 1982.
Schwager, Raymund. *Must There Be Scapegoats?* New York: Harper, 1987.

ARTHUR KIRSCH

Virtue, Vice, and Compassion in Montaigne and The Tempest

It has long been recognized that Shakespeare borrowed from Montaigne. Gonzalo's Utopian vision in *The Tempest* (II.i.142–76)[1] is indebted to a passage in Florio's translation of Montaigne's essay, "Of the Cannibals,"[2] and Prospero's speech affirming that "The rarer action is / In virtue than in vengeance" (V.i.20–32) is derived from the opening of Florio's translation of the essay, "Of Cruelty" (2:108). The king's speech in *All's Well That Ends Well* on the distinction between virtue and nobility (II.iii.117–44) appears to be a similarly direct, if less well-known, borrowing from "Upon Some Verses of Virgil" (3:72–3), an essay whose treatment of the polarization of sensuality and affection also has bearing upon *Othello*.[3] Leo Salingar has perspicuously shown that a number of the major themes of *King Lear*, as well as much of its distinctive vocabulary, are drawn from "An Apology of *Raymond Sebond*" and "Of the Affection of Fathers to their Children" as well as other essays;[4] and D. J. Gordon brilliantly demonstrated analogies between the critical stress upon names in *Coriolanus* and Montaigne's essay, "Of Glory."[5] Finally, as Robert Ellrodt has argued, the inward characterizations of Hamlet as well as of many of Shakespeare's other tragic heroes show clear affinities with the dynamics of self-consciousness, "a simultaneous awareness of experience and the experiencing self,"[6] that is fundamental to

From *Studies in English Literature, 1500–1900* 37, no. 2 (Spring 1997): 337–52. Copyright © 1997 by Rice University.

Montaigne's quest in all his essays to represent what he called "le passage" (3:23), the "minute to minute" movement of his mind.

The Tempest, however, remains the work in which Shakespeare's relation to Montaigne is most palpable and most illuminating. Shakespeare's play, of course, is exceptionally elusive. A variety of models and analogues have been proposed for it—Roman comedy, the Jacobean masque, and voyage literature among them—but it has no single, governing source to offer a scaffold for interpretation, and it remains in many ways as ineffable as Ariel's songs. Confronted with such suggestiveness, and in revolt against the apparent sentimentality of traditional readings, the disposition of most critics of the last two decades has been to follow W. H. Auden's lead in *The Sea and the Mirror* (1942–44)[7] and stress ironic and subversive ambiguities in the play as well as its apparently patriarchal and colonialist assumptions.[8]

Shakespeare's demonstrable borrowings from Montaigne in *The Tempest*, which are among the very few verifiable sources for the play, can provide a complementary, and I think more spacious, way of understanding *The Tempest*'s ambiguities. In the absence of a narrative source, Shakespeare's organization of the action, as well as Prospero's, seems unusually informed by the kind of working out of ideas that suggests the tenor of Montaigne's thinking: inclusive; interrogative rather than programmatic; anti-sentimental but humane; tragicomic rather than only tragic or comic, incorporating adversities rather than italicizing them as subversive ironies. The particular constellation of ideas in the play, moreover—the mutual dependence of virtue and vice, forgiveness, compassion, imagination—is habitual in Montaigne.

Of the two clear borrowings from Montaigne in *The Tempest*, Gonzalo's vision of Utopia is by far the most well-known and most discussed, but it is the play's more neglected relation to "Of Cruelty" as well as several associated essays that is more fundamental and that I wish mainly to focus upon in this essay. Montaigne remarks in "Of Cruelty" that "If vertue cannot shine but by resisting contrarie appetites, shall we then say, it cannot passe without the assistance of vice, and oweth him this, that by his meanes it attaineth to honour and credit" (2:110). He elaborates on the same theme in "Of Experience": "Even as the Stoickes say, *that Vices were profitably brought in; to give esteeme and make head unto vertue;* So may we with better reason and bold conjecture, affirme, that Nature hath lent us griefe and paine, for the honour of pleasure and service of indolency" (3:357). He also writes in "Of Experience," in a passage drawn from Plutarch: "Our life is composed, as is the harmony of the World, of contrary things; so of divers tunes, some pleasant, some harsh, some sharpe, some flat, some low and some high: What would that Musition say, that should love but some one of them? He ought to know how to use them severally and how to entermingle them. So should we both of goods and evils, which are consubstantiall to our life. Our being cannot subsist without this commixture, whereto one side is no lesse necessary than the other" (3:352–3).

Such a view of virtue's dependence on vice—paradoxical rather than invidiously binary—is clearly relevant to both the structure and texture of *The Tempest*. Antonio and Sebastian's unregenerate rapaciousness and desperation are contrasted throughout to Gonzalo's beneficence and hopefulness, quite directly during the very speech in which Gonzalo paraphrases Montaigne. Venus is counterpointed with Ceres within the wedding masque, and the conspiracy of Caliban, Stephano, and Trinculo complements as well as disrupts the performance of the masque itself, whose high artifice and graciousness remain in our memory as much as the drunken malice of the conspiracy does in Prospero's. Caliban's own earthiness is constantly in counterpoint to Ariel's spirit—they are conceived in terms of each other.

Similarly, Miranda's celebrated verse, "O brave new world / That has such people in't," is not denied by, but co-exists with, Prospero's answer, "'Tis new to thee" (V.i.183–4). Neither response is privileged: youth and age are as consubstantial in the play as good and evil. Prospero's skepticism is directed toward the court party Miranda admires, not toward her and Ferdinand, whose marriage he himself speaks of with reverence and hope:

> Fair encounter
> Of two most rare affections! Heavens rain grace
> On that which breeds between 'em.
>   (III.i.72–4)

The marriage, indeed, is at the heart of Prospero's "project" within the play and is finally associated with the "project" of the play itself, "Which was to please," that the actor playing Prospero refers to in the Epilogue.

Both projects depend upon a union of opposites, of goods and evils, that ultimately suggests transformation as well as symbiosis. At the outset of the action Prospero tells Miranda, when she sees the shipwreck, that there is "no harm done . . . No harm," and that he has "done nothing but in care" of her (I.ii.15–7). His care culminates in Miranda's betrothal, but evolves through her suffering as well as his own, and he associates that suffering with the blessing as well as pain of their exile from Milan. They were driven from the city, he tells her, "By foul play," but "blessedly holp hither" (I.ii.62–3):

> There they hoist us
> To cry to th' sea that roared to us, to sigh
> To th' winds, whose pity, sighing back again,

Did us but loving wrong.
    (I.ii.148–51)

The same motif is expressed by Ferdinand as he submits to Prospero's rule
and works as a "patient log-man" (III.i.68), a ritual ordeal that Prospero
contrives to make him earn and value the love of Miranda:

> There be some sports are painful, and their labour
> Delight in them set off, some kinds of baseness
> Are nobly undergone; and my most poor matters
> Point to rich ends. This my mean task
> Would be as heavy to me, as odious, but
> The mistress which I serve quickens what's dead,
> And makes my labours pleasures. O, she is
> Ten times more gentle than her father's crabbed,
> And he's composed of harshness. I must remove
> Some thousands of these logs and pile them up,
> Upon a sore injunction. My sweet mistress
> Weeps when she sees me work, and says such baseness
> Had never like executor. I forget.
> But these sweet thoughts do even refresh my labours,
> Most busil'est when I do it.
>   (III.i.1–15)

This paradoxical combination of opposites—delight and pain, gentleness
and harshness, the quickening of the dead—is analogous to the Christian idea
of *felix culpa* that nourished Guarini's conception of the genre of tragicomedy to
which *The Tempest* belongs and that is also to be found in the voyage literature
frequently associated with *The Tempest*.[9] In "A true reportory of the wreck" off
the islands of Bermuda, for example, William Strachey exalted the marvelous
beneficence of the shipwreck at the same time that he delineated the vicious
dissension among the voyagers that developed in Bermuda and later in Virginia,
the result, he wrote, of "the permissive providence of God."[10]

    The manner in which the possibility of fortunate suffering informs the
moral consubstantiality of the action of *The Tempest*, however, suggests the
particular force of the process of Montaigne's thought in the play, a process
that reaches its climax in Prospero's forgiveness of his enemies, the speech
that Shakespeare derived directly from "Of Cruelty." In the ostensibly digres-
sive manner that is typical of him, Montaigne opens the essay with a discussion of virtue, the passage Shakespeare paraphrases in the play. "Me thinks
vertue is another manner of thing," Montaigne writes,

and much more noble than the inclinations unto goodnesse, which in us are ingendered. Mindes well borne, and directed by themselves, follow one same path, and in their actions represent the same visage, that the vertuous doe. But vertue importeth, and soundeth somewhat I wot not what greater and more active, than by an happy complexion, gently and peaceably, to suffer it selfe to be led or drawne, to follow reason. He that through a naturall facilitie, and genuine mildnesse, should neglect or contemne injuries received, should no doubt performe a rare action, and worthy commendation: But he who being toucht and stung to the quicke, with any wrong or offence received, should arme himselfe with reason against this furiously-blind desire of revenge, and in the end after a great conflict, yeeld himselfe master over-it, should doubtlesse doe much more. The first should doe well, the other vertuously: the one action might be termed goodnesse, the other vertue. For, *It seemeth that the verie name of vertue presupposeth difficultie, and inferreth resistance, and cannot well exercise it seife without an enemie.* It is peradventure the reason we call God good, mightie, liberall, and just, but we terme him not vertuous.

(2:108)[11]

Shakespeare's version of this passage occurs in the last act of *The Tempest*, after Ariel tells Prospero of the sufferings of the court party.

Ariel. Your charm so strongly works 'em
That if you now beheld them, your affections
Would become tender.
Prospero. Dost thou think so, spirit?
Ariel. Mine would, sir, were I human.
Prospero. And mine shall.
Hast thou, which art but air, a touch, a feeling
Of their afflictions, and shall not myself,
One of their kind, that relish all as sharply
Passions as they, be kindlier moved than thou art?
Though with their high wrongs I am struck to th' quick,
Yet with my nobler reason 'gainst my fury
Do I take part. The rarer action is
In virtue than in vengeance. They being penitent,
The sole drift of my purpose doth extend
Not a frown further. Go, release them, Ariel.

My charms I'll break, their senses I'll restore,
And they shall be themselves.
   (V.i.17–32)

Shakespeare's reliance upon Florio's translation of Montaigne in this speech was first pointed out by Eleanor Prosser in 1965 and now seems self-evident.[12] "Though with their high wrongs I am struck to th' quick / Yet with my nobler reason 'gainst my fury / Do I take part" is clearly indebted in phraseology as well as conception to Montaigne, and "The rarer action is / In virtue than in vengeance" is particularly indebted to Florio's phrase, "performe a rare action," which in the original reads "feroit chose très-belle et digne de louange," "do a fine and praiseworthy thing." These verbal parallels have been generally accepted in Shakespeare criticism, but their larger implications for the characterization of Prospero and for much else in the play have been, I think, almost willfully neglected.[13] A figure of supernatural as well as patriarchal authority, Prospero has godlike attributes, including a disquieting measure of the kind of irritability and wrath that often characterizes the Lord God in the earlier books of the Old Testament, but he learns about his humanity in the course of the action,[14] and he transforms himself (as well as others) in a way that Montaigne specifically illuminates. His speech on compassion constitutes both an implicit acknowledgment of the difference between God's power and man's, a prologue to the adjuration of his "rough magic" that immediately follows, and an elucidation of the consequent strife that his human virtue entails. Many, if not most, of the traits and actions that in recent years have been thought to falsify Prospero's ostensible motives and to signify his intractably tyrannical, if not colonialist, mentality, are made immediately intelligible by Montaigne's essay. His impatience with his daughter, and with her suitor, the son of his enemy, his "beating mind," his insistent asperity, his marked reluctance in forgiving his brother, and his violence to Caliban: all are ultimately signs of the struggle of virtue that Montaigne describes. Rather than subverting Prospero's "project," they constitute and authenticate it. Touched and stung to the quick in the present as well as in the past, animated by a "furious," if not "furiously-blind desire of revenge," Prospero "in the end after a great conflict, yeeld[s] himselfe master over-it" (2:108). The emotional keynote of the play is precisely this sense of Prospero's labor pains, of the "sea-change," to paraphrase Ariel's luminous song, that he "suffer[s],"[15] of his "groan[ing]" "Under [the] burthen" of his "sea-sorrow" (I.ii.401, 156, 170) to give birth to new and resolved feelings. The action of the play dramatizes this process. The ordeals to which Prospero subjects others on the island are at once recapitulations of his beating memories and images of his effort to overcome them. His interruption of the wedding masque when he remembers Caliban (and perhaps thereby unconsciously expresses the threat of his own sexual desires)[16] is intelligible in just these terms, as is his ultimate and pained recognition that Caliban is native to him, has been made, indeed, partly in his image: "this thing of darkness I / Acknowledge mine" (V.i.275–6). The play's unusual obedience to the classical unities intensifies the sense of Prospero's struggle and is exactly appropriate to the presentation of the minute-to-minute pulsations, *le passage*, of a mind in the throes of accepting and forgiving.

Shakespeare also explores what makes compassion possible in *The Tempest*, and the whole of "Of Cruelty" is germane to this exploration, not just the introductory passage from which Shakespeare directly borrows. In the subsequent argument of the essay Montaigne reiterates the proposition that to be "simply stored with a facile and gentle nature" may "make a man innocent, but not vertuous," a condition "neere unto imperfection and weaknesse," and adds that "the verie names of Goodnesse and innocentie are for this respect in some sort names of contempt" (2:113). He goes on, however, to identify his own temperament with precisely such "a facile and gentle nature," and this identification is the essay's core subject. It is what makes the whole of it coherent, what connects it with "Of the Cannibals," whose essential subject is also cruelty,[17] and what forms the deepest ligament, I think, between both essays and Shakespeare's *Tempest*. "My vertue," Montaigne writes, "is a vertue, or to say better innocencie, accidentall and casuall . . . a kinde of simple-plaine innocencie, without vigor or art." "Amongst all other vices," he continues, announcing the theme of this essay, "there is none I hate more, than crueltie, both by nature and judgement, as the extremest of all vices" (2:115, 117). Montaigne's conjunction of his "innocence" and his hatred of cruelty has wide implications for an understanding of *The Tempest*. Montaigne says that he "cannot chuce but grieve" at seeing a "chickins neck puld off, or a pigge stickt," and "cannot well endure a seele dew-bedabled hare to groane, when she is seized upon by the houndes; although hunting be a violent sport" (2:117). His response is the same to cruelty to human beings. He protests that "Let any man be executed by law, how deservedly soever, I cannot endure to behold the execution with an unrelenting eye," and he condemns the "extreme point whereunto the crueltie of man may attaine," in which men torture others "onely to this end, that they may enjoy the pleasing spectacle." "I live in an age," he continues, "wherein we abound with incredible examples of this vice, through the licentiousnesse of our civill and intestine warres: And read all ancient stories, be they never so tragicall, you shall find not to equall those, we see daily practised" (2:119, 121). The contemporary civil wars in France elicit Montaigne's compassion, but they do not create it. The premise as well as the conclusion of Montaigne's response to cruelty is the recognition of his own inherently sympathetic nature: "I have a verie feeling and tender compassion of other mens afflictions, and should more easily weep for companie sake, if possiblie for any occasion whatsoever, I could shed teares. There is nothing sooner moveth teares in me, than to see others weepe, not onely fainedly, but howsoever, whether truly or forcedly" (2:119).

The discrimination of such compassionate impulses lies close to the heart of Montaigne's definition of himself in the *Essais* as a whole. In an addition made in 1588 to the opening essay of the first volume, when the full direction of the *Essais* must have become clear to him, he announces, "I am much inclined to mercie, and affected to mildnesse. So it is, that in mine opinion, I should more naturally stoope unto compassion, than bend to estimation. Yet is pitty held a vicious passion among the Stoicks. They would have us aid the afflicted, but not to faint, and co-suffer with them" (1:18). This opposition between compassion and detachment, as Jean Starobinski has suggested,[18] is part of the central dialectic of the *Essais*. Montaigne goes on to deprecate his mildness as effeminate and childish, but the Stoic self-sufficiency that at once animates his project and is its ostensible goal is always balanced, in this essay and in the *Essais* as a whole, by his disposition to sympathize and "co-suffer" with others. One critic has argued that in "[p]utting cruelty first" among vices, ahead even of the seven deadly sins, Montaigne in effect repudiates Christian theology.[19] But that issue is at least open to debate. Montaigne has plenty to say about pride in *Sebond* and elsewhere, and his extraordinary capacity to "co-suffer" with other human beings, remarkable for his age, but not unlike Shakespeare's, can just as aptly and interestingly be understood as an internalization, if not embodiment, of Christian charity.

In *The Tempest*, in any event, cosuffering, compassion, is a tonic chord in the whole of the action, not just the work of Prospero alone. It is revealed throughout the play in the "piteous heart" of Miranda, who is animated by "the very virtue of compassion," as well as in Gonzalo. Gonzalo's "innocence," like Miranda's, is "simple-plaine . . . without vigor or art," and like Montaigne's also, it is composed of a "verie feeling and tender compassion of others mens affliction" (2:117, 119). It is the sight of "the good old Lord Gonzalo" and others in tears, "Brimful of sorrow and dismay" (V.i.14–5), that prompts Ariel's sympathy for the courtiers, and through him, the movement toward compassion in Prospero. "[I]f you now beheld them, your affections / Would become tender," Ariel says to Prospero, "Mine would, sir, were I human" (V.i.18–9). And Prospero answers, as we have seen, that if Ariel, who is but air, can have a "feeling / Of their afflictions," shall not he, "One of their kind," who relishes passions as sharply as they, be "kindlier moved," take the part of "reason 'gainst [his] fury," and find the rarer action in virtue than in vengeance (V.i.21–6).

Prospero, of course, emphatically does not have the innocence that nourishes Miranda's "virtue of compassion," nor does he have the innocent nature of Gonzalo, though he has from the first understood and responded to both. They can forgive instinctively, he cannot. But in this speech, the decisive moment in the action, Prospero is able to emulate them. He speaks of his reason in the struggle of virtue, as Montaigne does, but the speech more importantly suggests another faculty as well. "Kind," as often in Shakespeare, denotes humankind as well as human kindness, and it is in the first instance Prospero's ability to imagine what others feel and to understand what he has in common with them—including, especially, Caliban—that enables him to sympathize with Alonso and to forgive Antonio and Sebastian despite the wrongs that continue to anger him.

It is particularly significant that it should be Ariel, associated throughout the play with Prospero's imaginative power, who prompts this movement, because human imagination is finally the deepest preoccupation of Shakespeare in *The Tempest* and a central filament in Montaigne's thoughts on compassion as well. In an apparent digression in the midst of the discussion of forgiveness in "Of Cruelty," Montaigne suggests that a lack of imagination can "*sometimes counterfeit vertuous effects*" and that the Germans and the Swiss, for example, appear brave in war because they have "scarce sense and wit" to imagine their danger, whereas the "subtiltie of the Italians, and the vivacitie of their conceptions" is so great, that they foresee "such dangers as might betide them . . . far-off" and can provide for their safety even before they actually see the danger (2:114). Montaigne's remark may be ironic, but it is nonetheless to such "sense and wit," such "vivacitie" of imagination, that he relates his own innocence and susceptibility to the suffering of others.

That imaginative susceptibility also subsumes the indictment of the cruelty of European culture in "Of the Cannibals," and it appears as well in interesting ways in another essay, "Of Cato the Younger," in which Montaigne writes,

> I am not possessed with this common errour, to judge of others according to that I am my selfe. I am easie to beleeve things differing from my selfe. Though I be engaged to one forme, I doe not tie the world unto it, as every man doth? And I beleeve and conceive a thousand manners of life, contrarie to the common sort: I more easily admit and receive difference, than resemblance in us. I discharge as much as a man will, another being of my conditions and principles, and simply consider of it my selfe without relation, framing it upon it's owne modell. Though my selfe be not continent, yet doe I sincerely commend and allow the continencie of the

Capuchins and Theatines, and highly praise their course of life. I
doe by imagination insinuate my selfe into their place: and by how
much more they bee other than my selfe, so much the more doe I
love and honour them.

(1:243)

Montaigne discusses an analogous imaginative "insinuation" in "Of
Diverting and Diversions," where he relates cosuffering to the creation as
well as effects of rhetoric and art:

An orator (saith Rhetorick) in the play of his pleading, shall be
moved at the sound of his owne voice, and by his fained agitations:
and suffer himselfe to be cozoned by the passion he representeth:
imprinting a lively and essentiall sorrow, by the jugling he acteth, to
transferre it into the judges, whom of the two it concerneth lesse:
As the persons hired at our funerals who to aide the ceremony of
mourning, make sale of their teares by measure, and of their sorrow
by waight . . . *Quintilian* reporteth, to have seene Comedians so
farre ingaged in a sorowful part, that they wept after being come
to their lodgings: and of himselfe, that having undertaken to move
a certaine passion in another: he had found himselfe surprised not
only with shedding of teares, but with a palenesse of countenance,
and behaviour of a man truly dejected with griefe.

(3:59–60)

Quintilian's remark is a commonplace of the period, but Montaigne's mention of it in "Of Diversions" has a special suggestiveness because, like *The
Tempest*, the essay associates the virtue of compassion not only with the
salutary effects of the imagination but also with its illusoriness.[20] Right after
mentioning Quintilian, Montaigne remarks that no cause is needed

to excite our minde. A doating humour without body, without
substance overswayeth and tosseth it up and downe. Let me
thinke of building Castles in *Spayne*, my imagination will forge
me commodities and afford me meanes and delights where-with
my minde is really tickled and essentially gladded. How ofte do
we pester our spirits with anger or sadnesse by such shadowes, and
entangle our selves into fantasticall passions which alter both our
mind and body? what astonished, flearing and confused mumpes
and mowes doth this dotage stirre up in our visages? what skippings
and agitations of members and voice, seemes it not by this man

alone, that he hath false visions of a multitude of other men with whom he doth negotiate; or some inwarde Goblin that torments him? Enquire of your selfe, where is the object of this alteration? Is there any thing but us in nature, except subsisting nullity? over whom it hath any power?

(3:61)

In a well-known passage in "An Apology of *Raymond Sebond*," Montaigne remarks that "We wake sleeping, and sleep waking. . . . Our reason and soul, receiving the phantasies and opinions, which sleeping seize on them, and authorising our dreames actions, with like approbation, as it doth the daies. Why make we not a doubt, whether our thinking, and our working be another dreaming, and our waking some kind of sleeping" (2:317).

The same consciousness both of the force of human imagination and of its evanescence in human existence haunts Shakespeare's *Tempest* as well. Caliban expresses it with the greatest immediacy in his moving speech about the magic of the island and of his own dreams:

Be not afeard, the isle is full of noises,
Sounds, and sweet airs, that give delight and hurt not.
Sometimes a thousand twangling instruments
Will hum about mine ears; and sometimes voices,
That if I then had waked after long sleep,
Will make me sleep again, and then in dreaming
The clouds methought would open and show riches
Ready to drop upon me, that when I waked
I cried to dream again.
    (III.ii.133–41)

Prospero conveys a similar apprehension of imaginative impalpability and wonder, in a more metaphysical key, in his famous speech to Ferdinand after the interruption of the masque. He is enraged with Caliban, but in that very process, he incorporates Caliban's dreaming as well as interprets it. "You do look, my son, in a moved sort," he tells Ferdinand,

As if you were dismayed. Be cheerful, sir;
Our revels now are ended. These our actors,
As I foretold you, were all spirits, and
Are melted into air, into thin air,
And, like the baseless fabric of this vision,
The cloud-capped towers, the gorgeous palaces,

The solemn temples, the great globe itself,
Yea, all which it inherit, shall dissolve,
And, like this insubstanial pageant faded,
Leave not a rack behind. We are such stuff
As dreams are made on, and our little life
Is rounded with a sleep.
    (IV.i.146–58)

The *topos* of life as a dream is of course very common in the Renaissance, but its collocation in *The Tempest* with the impalpable realities of the imagination as well as with Prospero's achievement of compassion, suggests the particular matrix of ideas found in Montaigne's essays. If not a source, Montaigne's association of these ideas is an explanation. One tendency in recent criticism of *The Tempest* has been to see Prospero's magnificent speech and the play itself as an expression of Shakespeare's disenchantment with the limitations of theatrical illusion.[21] But Caliban's dreaming and Prospero's incorporation of it in his reflection on the "baseless fabric of this vision" do not so much question the value of the theater, as characterize the dream-like nature of the human experience it imitates; and what the analogues to Montaigne should make clear is that Shakespeare's sense of this insubstantial pageant, of the subsisting nullity both of human existence and of the theater, is not ironic, but the "stuff" of wonder and a motive to charity.

The idea of imaginative insinuation and compassion is given a final, hauntingly expansive, turn in the epilogue to *The Tempest*, when Prospero, still the character but now also an ordinary human being, an actor, asks the audience for applause. He speaks at precisely the moment in a play when we too are midway between our own world and the world of the theater.[22] "Let me not," he says to us,

Since I have my dukedom got,
And pardoned the deceiver, dwell
In this bare island by your spell,
But release me from my bands
With the help of your good hands.
Gentle breath of yours my sails
Must fill, or else my project fails,
Which was to please. Now I want
Spirits to enforce, art to enchant;
And my ending is despair
Unless I be relieved by prayer,
Which pierces so that it assaults

Mercy itself, and frees all faults.
As you from crimes would pardoned be,
Let your indulence set me free.
      (V.i.323–38)

Jan Kott[23] as well as other critics and directors have wished to place the entire stress in this epilogue on "despair." The emphasis is more naturally placed, if we attend to the syntax, on the "piercing" power of prayer, a phraseology common in Shakespeare but never in this self-consciously theatrical context. Montaigne, very appositely, uses the word "pierce" in his essay, "Of the Force of the Imagination," to describe his vulnerability to the suffering of others: "I am one of those that feels a very great conflict and power of imagination. . . . The impression of it pierceth me. . . . The sight of others anguishes doth sensibly drive me into anguish; and my sense hath often usurped the sense of a third man" (1:92). The same thought and the same image of piercing inform Montaigne's description of the moving power of poetry, and especially of plays, in "Of Cato the Younger," the essay in which he talks of imaginatively insinuating himself into the place of others. "It is more apparently seene in theaters," he writes, "that the sacred inspiration of the Muses, having first stirred up the Poet with a kinde of agitation unto choler, unto griefe, unto hatred, yea and beyond himselfe, whither and howsoever they please, doth also by the Poet strike and enter into the Actor, and [consecutively] by the Actor, a whole auditorie or multitude. It is the ligament of our senses depending one of another." "Even from my infancie," he concludes, "Poesie hath had the vertue to transpierce and transport me" (1:246).

The religious reverberations of the allusion to the Lord's prayer in Prospero's epilogue may be peculiarly Shakespearean (though Montaigne too repeatedly identifies the verse "forgive us our trespasses" with the virtue of forgiveness), but the correspondences between the sympathetic illusions of the theater and of life, between theatrical imagination and human compassion, are essentially the same as they are in Montaigne. *The Tempest*, of course, calls attention to theatrical imagination not only in its evident meta-theatrical references but also in the distinctive manner in which it moves us. It begins with the depiction of a storm that captures Miranda's imaginative sympathy as well as ours, and then immediately makes us understand that the storm was not real, that it was an illusion of an illusion; and this exponential consciousness of our own imaginative work in the theater informs our response throughout the action. We are thus peculiarly receptive to Prospero's epilogue. For what the actor playing Prospero suggests, in his grave and beautiful plea for our applause, is a recapitulation and crystallization of what the experience of the play itself has all along induced us to feel: that the illusory and evanescent passions of the theater are like those of actual life, and that both can be cosuffered, that the imaginative sympathy which animates our individual responses to the play also binds us together, "our senses depending one of another." He suggests, in a plea which is like a prayer, that an audience's generosity to the fictions of the actors is like mercy itself, and that the compassionate imaginative ligaments which form a community within the theater can also compose a community, in Montaigne's words, "void of all revenge and free from all rancour" (1:365), outside of it. There is no more spacious and humane a justification of the theater in all of Shakespeare.[24]

Notes

1. All references to *The Tempest* are to the New Oxford edition, ed. Stephen Orgel (Oxford: Clarendon Press, 1987) and will be cited parenthetically in the text by act, scene, and line numbers.

2. *Montaigne's Essays*, trans. John Florio, ed. L. C. Harmer, 3 vols. (London: Everyman's Library-Dent, 1965), 1:220. Subsequent references to Montaigne's essays are to this edition and will be cited parenthetically in the text by volume and page number.

3. For a discussion of Shakespeare's affinities to Montaigne in *All's Well That Ends Well* and *Othello*, see Arthur Kirsch, *Shakespeare and the Experience of Love* (Cambridge: Cambridge Univ. Press, 1981), pp. 121–7, 38–9.

4. Leo Salingar, *Dramatic Form in Shakespeare and the Jacobeans* (Cambridge: Cambridge Univ. Press, 1986), pp. 107–33. See also Kenneth Muir, ed., New Arden edition of *King Lear* (Cambridge MA: Harvard Univ. Press, 1959), pp. 249–53.

5. D. J. Gordon, "Name and Fame: Shakespeare's *Coriolanus*," in *The Renaissance Imagination: Essays and Lectures by D. J. Gordon*, ed. Stephen Orgel (Berkeley and Los Angeles: Univ. of California Press, 1980), pp. 203–19.

6. Robert Ellrodt, "Self-Consciousness in Montaigne and Shakespeare," in *ShS* 28 (1975): 37–50, 42.

7. See also W. H. Auden's brilliant interpretation of *The Tempest* in *The Dyer's Hand and Other Essays* (New York: Random House, 1962), pp. 128–34.

8. For the most comprehensive and elegant instance of contemporary interpretations of *The Tempest*, see Stephen Orgel's introduction to his New Oxford edition of the play, pp. 1–87. For discussions of the subject of colonialism, specifically, see, e.g., Stephen J. Greenblatt, "Learning to Curse: Aspects of Linguistic Colonialism in the Sixteenth Century," in *First Images of America: The Impact of the New World on the Old*, ed. Fredi Chiapelli, vol. 2 (Berkeley and Los Angeles: Univ. of California Press, 1976), pp. 561–80; Francis Barker and Peter Hulme, "Nymphs and Reapers Heavily Vanish: The Discursive Contexts of *The Tempest*," in *Alternative Shakespeares*, ed. John Drakakis (London and New York: Methuen, 1985), pp. 191–205; Terence Hawkes, "Swisser-Swatter: Making a Man of English Letters," in *Alternative Shakespeares*, pp. 26–46; and Paul Brown, "'This thing of darkness I acknowledge mine': *The Tempest* and the Discourse of Colonialism," in *Political Shakespeare: New Essays in Cultural Materialism* (Ithaca and London: Cornell Univ. Press, 1985), pp. 48–71. For a full consideration of the scholarship on colonialism and *The Tempest* and a decisively trenchant criticism of it, see Meredith Anne Skura,

"Discourse and the Individual: The Case of Colonialism in *The Tempest*," *SQ* 40, 1 (Spring 1989): 42–69.

9. See Arthur C. Kirsch, *Jacobean Dramatic Perspectives* (Charlottesville: Univ. Press of Virginia, 1972), pp. 7–15.

10. See, e.g., William Strachey, "A true repertory of the wreck," Appendix B, *The Tempest*, ed. Orgel, pp. 212–3.

11. "Il me semble que la vertu est chose autre et plus noble que les inclinations à la bonté qui naissent en nous. Les ame reglées d'elles mesmes et bien nées, elles suyvent mesme train, et representent en leurs actions mesme visage que les vertueuses. Mais la vertu sonne je ne sçay quoi de plus grand et de plus actif que de se laisser, par une heureuse complexion, doucement et paisiblement conduire à la suite de la raison. Celuy qui, d'une douceur et facilité naturelle, mespriseroit les offences receus, feroit chose très-belle et digne de louange; mais celuy qui, picqué et outré jusques au vif d'une offence, s'armeroit des armes de la raison contre ce furieux appetit de vengeance, et après un grand conflict s'en redroit en fin maistre, feroit sans doute beaucoup plus. Celuy-là feroit bien, et cettuy-cy vertuesement; l'une action se pourroit dire bonté; l'autre, vertu; car il semble que le nom de la vertu presuppose de la difficulté et du contraste, et qu'elle ne peut s'exercer sans partie. C'est à l'aventure pourquoy nous nommons Dieu bon, fort, et liberal, et juste; mais nous ne le nommons pas vertueux: ses operations sont toutes naifves et sans effort" (Michel Montaigne, *Oeuvres Complètes*, ed. Albert Thibaudet et Maurice Rat [Paris: Pléiade-Gallimard, 1962], pp. 400–1).

12. Eleanor Prosser, "Shakespeare, Montaigne, and the 'Rarer Action,'" *ShakS* 1 (1965): 261–4.

13. For a notable exception, see John B. Bender, "The Day of *The Tempest*," *ELH* 47, 2 (Summer 1980): 235–58, 250–1.

14. See Jack Miles, *God: A Biography* (New York: Alfred A. Knopf, 1995), pp. 240–4, for a suggestive discussion of the changing faces of God Himself in the Old Testament, including in Second Isaiah, the movement, through His participation in human experience, from an inhumane (because first inhuman) God to a God of "loving pity."

15. For an illuminating explication of Ariel's song and particularly the transformational resonance of the word "suffers," see Stephen Orgel, "New Uses of Adversity: Tragic Experience in *The Tempest*," in *In Defense of Reading: A Reader's Approach to Literary Criticism*, ed. Reuben A. Brower and Richard Poirier (New York: Dutton, 1962), pp. 110–32, 116.

16. See Skura, p. 60.

17. See David Quint, "A Reconsideration of Montaigne's *Des Cannibales*," *MLQ* 51, 4 (December 1990): 459–89. Quint argues that Montaigne is less interested in investigating the new world in "Des Cannibales" than in criticizing the old and concludes that Montaigne "may not so much create the figure of the noble savage" in the essay "as disclose the savagery of the nobility" (p. 482).

18. Jean Starobinski, *Montaigne in Motion*, trans. Arthur Goldhammer (Chicago and London: Univ. of Chicago Press, 1985).

19. Judith N. Shklar, *Ordinary Vices* (Cambridge MA and London: Harvard Univ. Press, 1984), pp. 7–44.

20. For a discussion from a different perspective of the possible relevance of "Of Diversions" to *The Tempest*, see Gail Kern Paster, "Montaigne, Dido, and *The Tempest*: 'How came that widow in?'" *SQ* 35, 1 (Spring 1984): 91–4.

21. See, e.g., Alvin B. Kernan, *The Playwright as Magician: Shakespeare's Image of the Poet in the English Public Theater* (New Haven and London: Yale Univ. Press, 1979), pp. 129–59.

22. See Michael Goldman, *Shakespeare and the Energies of Drama* (Princeton: Princeton Univ. Press, 1972), pp. 147–8.

23. Jan Kott, *Shakespeare Our Contemporary*, trans. Boleslaw Taborski (Garden City NY: Anchor Books–Doubleday, 1966), pp. 237–85.

24. An abbreviated version of this essay was presented in a talk at a symposium on "Cultural Exchange between European Nations" in Uppsala, Sweden and published in *Studia Acta Universitatis Upsaliensia Anglistica Upsaliensia 86*, ed. Gunnar Sorelius and Michael Srigley (Uppsala, 1994), pp. 111–21.

ALAN STEWART

'Near Akin': The Trials of Friendship
in The Two Noble Kinsmen

Critics have never been happy with *The Two Noble Kinsmen*.[1] It has traditionally been regarded as an unsatisfactory play, compromised, in Ann Thompson's words, by 'many tensions and inconsistencies';[2] to at least one critic, it remains 'that most distressing of plays'.[3] Despite its use of an archetypal story of two male friends brought into conflict over a woman, already tried and tested by Boccaccio (in the *Teseida*) and Chaucer (*Knight's Tale*), its telling here has seemed less than successful. Theodore Spencer went so far as to complain that the story of Palamon and Arcite 'is intrinsically feeble, superficial, and undramatic'.[4] The characters themselves have been 'dismissed as virtually interchangeable emblems of Platonic love and chivalric courtesy—Tweedledum and Tweedledee as Kenneth Muir once called them'.[5] Some have attributed this to the inherent contradictions of the play's genre, tragicomedy.[6] Some have attributed it to its collaborative authorship by Fletcher and Shakespeare, as if each playwright wrote in solitary ignorance of his partner's work, and the play necessarily betrayed that process.[7] This approach makes possible, for example, the argument that Shakespeare composed the first exchange between Palamon and Arcite, but that Fletcher was responsible for their apparently contradictory quarrel in the prison scene.[8]

From *Shakespeare's Late Plays: New Readings*, edited by Jennifer Richards and James Knowles, pp. 57–71. Copyright © 1999 by Edinburgh University Press.

In this chapter, I prefer to follow the approach of Richard Hillman, who has argued that 'it is . . . possible, especially in a post-modern critical climate, to take the play's internal jars, whatever their origin . . . as integral to the text we have, not as blocking the text that might have been'.[9] I shall argue that, rather than being a failed attempt at a play about idealised male friendship, *The Two Noble Kinsmen* is rather a play about a failed attempt at idealised male friendship. In turn, I shall suggest, this failure derives from the juxtaposition of both classical-humanist and chivalric modes of male friendship with the realities of social relations, and a particular form of kinship, in Jacobean England.

The Two Noble Kinsmen contains a proliferation of variations on that classical and then humanist theme of *amicitia*, the idealised male friendship celebrated in such key Renaissance pedagogical texts as Cicero's *De amicitia* and *De officiis* and Seneca's *De beneficiis*.[10] First, Theseus and Pirithous present an established example of *amicitia*, a legendary male couple revered alongside Orestes and Pylades, Damon and Pythias, and Scipio and Laelius. Pirithous operates to Theseus as *alter ipse*, another himself, to the extent that he stands in as Theseus at his friend's wedding to Hippolyta, because Theseus is honour-bound to avenge the deaths of the husbands of the three queens. In Emilia's words 'The one of th'other may be said to water / Their intertangled roots of love' (I, iii, 58–9).

Second, we encounter the female friendship of Emilia and Flavina. Emilia tells of her love for the innocent 'play-fellow' (I, iii, 50) of her childhood who died young:

> What she liked
> Was then of me approved; what not, condemned—
> No more arraignment. The flower that I would pluck
> And put between my breasts (then but beginning
> To swell about the blossom), oh, she would long
> Till she had such another, and commit it
> To the like innocent cradle, where phoenix-like
> They died in perfume.
>   (I, iii, 64–71)

This intense female friendship, located in early pubescence and now irretrievably lost, occupies the same elegiac space as those in earlier Shakespeare plays: Rosalind and Celia in *As You Like It*, and Helena and Hermia in *A Midsummer Night's Dream*, for example.[11]

But the central friendship is that of Palamon and Arcite. As they are imprisoned together, Arcite gives one of the most passionate friendship speeches in English literature:

And here being thus together,
We are an endless mine to one another;
We are one another's wife, ever begetting
New births of love; we are father, friends, acquaintance,
We are, in one another, families;
I am your heir and you are mine. This place
Is our inheritance; no hard oppressor
Dare take this from us; here, with a little patience,
We shall live long and loving.
   (II, ii, 78–86)

Palamon answers, 'Is there record of any two that loved / Better than we do, Arcite?', to which Arcite affirms, 'Sure there cannot.' 'I do not think it possible', continues Palamon, 'our friendship / Should ever leave us'. 'Till our deaths it cannot', declares Arcite, 'And after death our spirits shall be led / To those that love eternally' (II, ii, 112–17). The tale of Palamon and Arcite as told in this play thus echoes that quintessential humanist fiction of the two male friends, temporarily rent asunder by the intrusion of a woman, who then go on to make up, usually with one of them marrying the woman, and the other marrying his friend's sister. Perhaps the most famous example is the story of Titus and Gisippus, told by Boccaccio in his *Decameron*, and then Englished by Thomas Elyot, and placed centrally in his influential *Boke Named the Gouernour*.[12] The moral of such tales is that, despite the claims of family and marriage, male friendship will emerge as the supreme affective force in the lives of the two men.

This superabundance of friendships should, I suggest, raise our suspicions from the start, as couple after couple are introduced displaying apparently textbook adherence to the model. As Theodore Spencer wrote incisively in 1939, '[o]ne of Shakespeare's favourite dramatic devices in his mature work is to establish a set of values and then to show how it is violated by the individual action which follows'.[13] Here, these three instances are introduced precisely to point up the relative failings of two of them. In the case of Emilia and Flavina, the elegiac tone points to the futility of a female version of *amicitia*, always already lost. But more importantly, in Palamon and Arcite something is terribly wrong. From the declaration just quoted, the eternal friendship of Palamon and Arcite lasts exactly two more lines, by which time Palamon has caught sight of Emilia, and Arcite has to urge him (unsuccessfully) to 'forward' with his speech. Their subsequent quarrel over Emilia, leading to an illegal duel, and ultimately to the strange death of Arcite—rather than to the usual double marriage—indicates clearly that all is not well in this telling of their friendship.

The reason for this, I shall suggest, is that in Palamon and Arcite we see a literary, humanist template sitting uncomfortably on a particular Jacobean social reality. The story of Palamon and Arcite is subtly nuanced in each of its retellings. As Eugene Waith notes, in Boccaccio's *Teseida*, it is 'basically a tale of lovers'; in Chaucer's *Knight's Tale*, the relationship is a 'chivalric bond of blood-brotherhood'.[14] In Shakespeare and Fletcher's version, I suggest, Palamon and Arcite are, first and foremost, as the title makes quite clear, *kinsmen*, and as they constantly reiterate, *cousins*. In this chapter, I shall argue that we can make far more sense of *The Two Noble Kinsmen* if we stop thinking of it as a play about friendship, and approach it instead as a play about the problems of kinship, and specifically the problems of cognatic cousinage.[15]

The Two Noble Kinsmen operates, as much of Jacobean England operated, within a culture where women (and figuratively, their virginity) were passed between families in marriage for financial gain; in the upper middling classes and above, these transactions were often complex and lengthy affairs, as befitted such important exchanges of lands, goods and cash. From the first words of the prologue, *The Two Noble Kinsmen* situates itself centrally within such a culture:

> New plays and maidenhead are near akin:
> Much followed both, for both much money gi'en,
> If they stand sound and well. And a good play,
> Whose modest scenes blush on his marriage day
> And shake to lose his honour, is like her
> That after holy tie [the wedding] and first night's stir
> Yet still is Modesty and still retains
> More of the maid, to sight, than husband's pains.
>   (Prologue, ll. 1–8)

The action of the play is inserted into an interrupted marriage (once again, as in *A Midsummer Night's Dream*, Theseus and Hippolyta have to wait!); the action is concluded when Emilia is exchanged between her new brother-in-law Theseus and the surviving kinsman, Palamon. (Although Arcite appears to give Emilia to Palamon with his dying breath—'Take her. I die' (V, iv, 95)—in fact it is Theseus who endorses the match). Even the Jailor's Daughter becomes marriageable because Palamon, in gratitude for her actions in springing him from gaol, gives 'a sum of money to her marriage: / A large one'—a gift, of course, not directly to the woman, but to her father, in order that he might marry her to the advantage of both father and daughter (IV, i, 21–4). When Palamon and Arcite are imprisoned, they first bewail the fact that they must remain bachelors; as Arcite puts it:

here age must find us
And, which is heaviest, Palamon, unmarried.
The sweet embraces of a loving wife,
Loaden with kisses, armed with thousand Cupids,
Shall never clasp our necks; no issue know us;
No figures of ourselves shall we e'er see,
To glad our age, and like young eagles teach 'em
Boldly to gaze against bright arms and say,
'Remember what your fathers were, and conquer!'
(II, ii, 25–36)

Much critical work has been done to illuminate this commodification of women in marriage, most notably Gayle Rubin's reworking of the anthropological work of Claude Lévi-Strauss to uncover the 'traffic in women', and Eve Sedgwick's combining of this with René Girard's triangular formulation to reread male rivalry over women as the prime feature of male homosociality.[16] In her study of quattrocento and cinquecento Florence, Christiane Klapisch-Zuber has shown how these abstract structures operated in practice. 'In Florence', she writes, 'men *were* and *made* the "houses". The word *casa* designates . . . the material house, the lodging of a domestic unit. . . . But it also stands for an entire agnatic kinship group.' These houses, and kinship in general, were 'determined by men, and the male branching of genealogies drawn up by contemporaries shows how little importance was given, after one or two generations, to kinship through women'. She illustrates graphically how, as they married, women moved between houses—both lineage groups and the physical buildings—demonstrating both the stability of the house, and the radical discontinuity of the lives of the women exchanged between them:

> In these *case*, in the sense of both physical and the symbolic house, women were passing guests. To contemporary eyes, their movements in relation to the *case* determined their social personality more truly than the lineage group from which they came. It was by means of their physical 'entrances' and 'exits' into and out of the 'house' that their families of origin or of alliance evaluated the contribution of women to the greatness of the *casa*.[17]

Although the importance of kinship in the English middling classes is thought to have been diminishing during this period, in the upper classes it still held sway. As Keith Wrightson writes, '[i]t is undoubtedly true . . . that both the titular aristocracy and the upper gentry were deeply preoccupied

with ancestry and lineage and that they tended to recognise a wide range
of kinsmen';[18] indeed Anthony Fletcher has asserted that in Sussex county
society 'kinship was the dominant principle'.[19] Mervyn James writes that the
deepest obligation in any man's life was:

> to the lineage, the family and kinship group. For this, being inher-
> ited with the 'blood', did not depend on promise or oath. It could
> neither be contracted into, nor could the bond be broken. For a
> man's very being as honourable had been transmitted to him with
> the blood of his ancestors, themselves honourable men. Honour
> therefore was not merely an individual possession, but that of the
> collectivity, the lineage. Faithfulness to the kinship group arose
> out of this intimate involvement of personal and collective honour,
> which meant that both increased or diminished together. Conse-
> quently, in critical honour situations where an extremity of conflict
> arose, or in which dissident positions were taken up involving
> revolt, treason and rebellion, the ties of blood were liable to assert
> themselves with a particular power.[20]

Viewed in this English social context, rather than in its humanist literary
context, the play reads rather differently. The first words uttered by Arcite put
in place a competition between affective and familial links: 'Dear Palamon,
dearer in love than blood / And our prime cousin' (I, ii, 1–2). The 'love' that
Arcite feels for Palamon is greater than the claim of 'blood', the fact that they
are first cousins. Yet they refer to themselves constantly in kinship terms (at
least thirty-eight times in the course of the play): 'cousin', 'coz', 'noble cousin'
(II, ii, 1), 'gentle cousin' (II, ii, 70 and III, vi, 112), 'fair cousin' (III, vi, 18),
'sweet cousin' (III, vi, 69), 'Clear-spirited cousin' (I, ii, 74), 'My coz, my coz'
(III, i, 58), 'kinsman' (III, vi, 21), 'noble kinsman' (II, ii, 193 and III, vi, 17).[21]
Even when the two are estranged during their competition for Emilia, they
are 'Traitor kinsman' (III, i, 30) and 'base cousin' (III, iii, 44) and Palamon can
punningly answer Arcite's 'Dear cousin Palamon' with 'Cozener Arcite' (III, i,
43–4), reminding us that the root of 'cozening' is the cozener's claim to be his
victim's long-lost cousin.[22]

'Cousin', like 'kinsman', is a deliberately vague term in early modern
English, one that can refer to any loose family connection: Anthony Fletcher
writes that in Sussex, 'stress on cousinage in correspondence and account
keeping became a mere mark of courtesy. The tight circles of intimate friendship, which were more significant for the dynamics of country affairs, ran
within the wider circles of blood'.[23] But these men are not merely 'kinsmen':
they share a very particular relationship—to Theseus, they are 'royal german

foes' (V, i, 9), implying a close cousin relationship, and in the Herald's words, 'They are sisters' children, nephews to the King' (I, iv, 16). This echoes the Chaucerian source, where they are described as being 'of the blood riall / Of Thebes, and of sistren two yborne' (ll. 1018–19).[24] This point is reiterated strikingly as Palamon and Arcite go through the ritual motions before their attempted duel: Palamon asserts:

> Thou art mine aunt's son
> And that blood we desire to shed is mutual,
> In me thine and in thee mine.
> (III, vi, 94–6)

In other words, their blood relationship derives from the female line—in Roman or Scottish law terms, their kinship is *cognatic*, rather than *agnatic* (through the male line). Palamon and Arcite are an example, therefore, of what we might call 'cognatic cousinage'.

There is no doubting of course that the kin relationship of cousins german, or first cousins, is extremely close, so close that if one were male and one female, then their right to marry each other would be disputed. However, seen in terms of a culture that exchanges women between patriarchal houses, cousins german whose kinship is cognatic occupy a strangely distant relationship: they are necessarily born into different houses, because their mothers married into different houses. This means, then, that the connection between the two cousins is not necessarily mutually beneficial—what benefits one need not benefit the other.

The peculiarity of this particular kinship relationship—its intense affective claims belied by its signal lack of practical utility—can be glimpsed in the tortuous interactions of two contemporary cousins german: Sir Robert Cecil and Francis Bacon. Cecil was the son of William Cecil, Lord Burghley, by his second wife Mildred Cooke; Bacon was the son of Sir Nicholas Bacon, Lord Keeper, by his second wife Anne Cooke. Mildred and Anne were sisters, two of the renowned and learned daughters of Sir Anthony Cooke, and thus Robert and Francis were first cousins, an instance of cognatic cousinage. But this apparently close family connection was put under great strain after the premature death of Francis's father in February 1579. Left without adequate provision by his father, and unable to call on his estranged elder half-brothers after a dispute about the will, Francis naturally turned to his uncle, Lord Burghley. Throughout his correspondence of the 1580s and early 1590s there are unveiled hints that Burghley might want to become a surrogate parent to his poor nephew. Instead, however, Francis was to be consistently disappointed by his uncle, who put his energies behind his own son, and other protégés. Francis in turn was forced to look for support beyond his immediate family, and turned in 1588 to Elizabeth's new young favourite, Robert Devereux, the second earl of Essex.[25]

Essex backed Francis in his bid to become Attorney-General in 1593 and 1594. It soon became clear, however, that Burghley and Cecil were backing another candidate, Edward Coke. This situation produced some highly charged encounters between Bacon's supporters (including Essex and Bacon's mother) and Coke's supporters (Burghley and Cecil). Such an encounter is recorded for us by one of Essex's intelligencers, Anthony Standen, to whom Essex related the anecdote.[26] At the end of January 1593, in the privacy of a shared coach, Sir Robert asked Essex who his candidate was for the vacant post of Attorney-General. Essex affected astonishment, declaring that he 'wondered Sir Robert should ask him that question, seeing it could not be unknown unto him that resolutely against all whosoever for Francis Bacon he stood'.

Sir Robert affected amazement. 'Good Lord', he replied, 'I wonder your Lordship should go about to spend your strength in so unlikely or impossible a matter.' It was out of the question, he continued, that Francis Bacon should be raised to a position of such eminence, since he was simply too young and inexperienced (Francis was thirty-three at the time). Essex readily admitted that he could not think of a precedent for so youthful a candidate for the post of attorney. But he pointed out that youth and inexperience did not seem to be hindering the bid by Sir Robert himself ('[a] younger than Francis, of lesser learning and of no greater experience') to become principal secretary of state, the most influential of all government posts. Cecil retaliated immediately:

> I know your lordship means myself. Although my years and experience are small, yet weighing the school I studied in and the great wisdom and learning of my schoolmaster, and the pains and observations I daily passed, yet I deem my qualifications to be sufficient. The added entitlement of my father's long service will make good the rest.

Unconvinced, Essex passionately reaffirmed his support for Bacon. 'And for your own part Sir Robert', he concluded, 'I think strange both of my Lord Treasurer and you that can have the mind to seek the preferment of a stranger before so near a kinsman as a first cousin.'

This exchange demonstrates vividly both the symbolic and the practical implications of various relationships between kinsmen. It testifies to the real practical value of the closest kin relationships: Cecil's career is quite explicitly acknowledged as his birthright, because of his father's success. Cognatic cousinage, however, is more complex. On the one hand, we see here the social expectations of the relationship, and of its powerful affective pull ('strange [that] you . . . can have the mind to seek the preferment of a stranger before so near a kinsman as a first cousin'). On the other, we witness the ineffectiveness of this claim in practical terms: Burghley and Cecil are never swayed to support Bacon (Bacon was not to reach public office for another twelve years, and his career only took off following Cecil's death in 1612). Although the situation was thought unfair by many, Bacon had no legal or moral claim on his cognatic relatives.

The Two Noble Kinsmen is not about either of the cousins' attempting to use the other in any practical sense. As Jeffrey Masten has pointed out, their similarity, a standard trope of *amicitia* literature, is indeed deployed to suggest that they will inevitably enter into competition:

ARCITE.   . . . am not I
Part of your blood, part of your soul? You have told me
That I was Palamon, and you were Arcite.
PALAMON. Yes.
ARCITE. Am not I liable to those affections,
Those joys, griefs, angers, fears, my friend shall suffer?
      (II, ii, 187–91)[27]

However, the futility of their kinship is signalled throughout the play by a skilfully maintained figurative representation. As the chapters in this collection by Helen Hackett and Gordon McMullan amply illustrate, the late plays return insistently to figures of maternity and manliness. These two sisters' sons, who, as we have already seen, describe themselves as their aunts' sons, are constantly referred to in terms of their mothers. When asked what she thinks of Arcite, Emilia answers that 'Believe, / His mother was a wondrous handsome woman; / His face, methinks, goes that way' (II, v, 19–21) (although Hippolyta then contends that 'his body / And fiery mind illustrate a brave father' (II, v, 21–2)). Later Emilia describes Palamon as being 'swart and meagre, of an eye as heavy / As if he had lost his mother' (IV, ii, 27–8). Together, she insists, 'Two greater and two better never yet / Made mothers joy' (IV, ii, 63–4). When Palamon berates the kind of men who boast of their sexual conquests, those 'large confessors', he 'hotly ask[s] them / If they had mothers—I had one, a woman, / And women 'twere they wronged' (V, i, 105–7). To Palamon the image of womanhood is his mother.

Firmly established as mothers' boys, the masculinity of both Palamon and Arcite is steadily chipped away throughout the play by a number of analogies, several with Ovidian overtones: as Jonathan Bate argues, '[c]ollaboration with Ovid is one of the marks of Fletcher and Shakespeare's collaboration with each other'.[28] When they are in prison, delineating their *amicitia*, Arcite exclaims that 'We are one another's wife, ever begetting / New births of love' (II, ii, 80–1). Two classical archetypes of passive male sexuality, Narcissus and Ganymede, are reiterated. Immediately after Arcite and Palamon assert their status as wives to each other, Emilia picks some narcissus from the garden, asserting that 'That was a fair boy certain, but a fool / To love himself. Were there not maids enough?' (II, ii, 120–2), referring of course to the myth of Narcissus dying while longing for his own reflection, having rejected the women who loved him. The connection is made explicit when Emilia later compares pictures of her two suitors—Palamon may be to Arcite 'mere dull shadow; /. . . . swart and meagre, of an eye as heavy':

> As if he had lost his mother; a still temper;
> No stirring in him, no alacrity;
> Of all this sprightly sharpness, not a smile.
> Yet these that we count errors may become him:
> Narcissus was a sad boy, but a heavenly.
>   (IV, ii, 26–32)

As the work of James Saslow, Leonard Barkan and Bruce R. Smith has shown, Ganymede had become by the Renaissance a standard figure for sodomitical, and specifically passive sodomitical, identification.[29] In the same speech, Emilia compares Arcite to Ganymede, one of the 'prettie boyes / That were the darlinges of the gods'. In Golding's words:

> The king of Gods [Jupiter] did burne ere while in loue of *Ganymed*
> The *Phrygian*, and the thing was found which *Iupiter* that sted,
> Had rather be then that he was. Yet could he not beteeme
> The shape of any other bird than Eagle for to seeme:
> And so he soring in the ayre with borrowed wings trust vp
> The *Troiane* boy, who stil in heauen euen yet doth beare his cup,
> And brings him *Nectar*, though against Dame *Iunos* wil it bee.[30]

Emilia declares:

>   What an eye,
> Of what a fiery spark and quick sweetness,
> Has this young prince! Here Love himself sits smiling;
> Just such another wanton Ganymede
> Set Jove afire with, and enforced the god

Snatch up the goodly boy, and set him by him,
A shining constellation. What a brow,
Of what a spacious majesty, he carries,
Arched like the great-eyed Juno's, but far sweeter,
Smoother than Pelops' shoulder!
    (IV, ii, 12–21)

We move from the beautiful shepherd boy Ganymede snatched up to become Jove's cupbearer in the heavens, to Jove's own wife Juno, to the ivory shoulder that replaced the shoulder of Pelops served up by his father Tantalus (and as ever, we are not sure here whether the smooth shoulder is the succulent one eaten, or the ivory replacement).[31] Palamon and Arcite are led through a serious of analogies that cast them as women, or as passive male bodies eaten by men or made love to by men, or as men in love with their own reflection. These images multiply through the play, and no amount of recognition for Arcite's potential prowess as a wrestler is going to shake them off.

What effect might this have on a reading of *The Two Noble Kinsmen*? I return to the speech I quoted earlier, where Palamon and Arcite pledge eternal friendship. It is indeed a remarkable and passionate speech, but we need to see it in context. It comes during the couple's imprisonment: at the beginning of the scene (II, ii), Palamon bewails their situation ('Oh, cousin Arcite, / Where is Thebes now? Where is our noble country? / Where are our friends and kindred?' (II, ii, 6–8)) and Arcite agrees that their 'hopes are prisoners with us' (II, ii, 26), lamenting the fact that they will never marry, nor have children, nor hunt again. It is only then that Arcite exclaims:

    Yet, cousin,
Even from the bottom of these miseries,
From all that Fortune can inflict upon us,
I see two comforts rising, two mere blessings,
If the gods please: to hold here a brave patience
And the enjoying of our griefs together.
While Palamon is with me, let me perish
If I think this our prison!
    (II, ii, 55–62)

Palamon replies:

    Certainly,
'Tis a main goodness, cousin, that our fortunes
Were twined together; 'tis most true, two souls

Put in two noble bodies, let 'em suffer
The gall of hazard, so they grow together,
Will never sink; they must not, say they could.
A willing man dies sleeping and all's done.
  (II, ii, 62–8)

It is then that they go on to 'make this prison holy sanctuary / To keep us from corruption of worse men' (II, ii, 71–2), and go into their passionate speech of friendship. As this preamble shows, however, the speech is a set piece, arrived at only after despair has cast them down, and as a pragmatic response to their dire situation. Friendship in the classic Ciceronian mould is only an option once imprisonment takes away their social agency. It does not stand up to comparison with the successful friendship of Theseus and Pirithous, or with the elegaic friendship of Emilia and Flavina, which have been carefully set up before precisely to demonstrate the failings of Palamon and Arcite's friendship; the first oblique comment on their declaration of friendship is Emilia's discussion of Narcissus. And even within the speech just quoted we can sense something awry: these two friends are 'two souls / Put in two noble bodies' (II, ii, 64–5), when the classic formulation of friendship is a single soul in two bodies. The hyperbole of being each other's wife, family, heir is merely a response to the deprivation of social agency; the minute that a way back into the real world is spied (in the form of Emilia, marriage to whom will ensure not only freedom but social success in Athens) the eternal friendship is shelved.

While the influence of Ciceronian *amicitia* is evident throughout, the play's immediate source requires that the authors also deal with the male friendship associated with chivalric codes. Here again, all is not as it might be. Chaucer's *Knight's Tale* has an ending which can still be seen as happy within the expectations of its genre: one knight wins his lady in honourable chivalric contest, but dies in an accident; after a suitable period, the lady is granted to the honourable loser. Much has been written about the chivalric elements of *The Two Noble Kinsmen*: it has been seen as linked to a neo-chivalric movement associated with Prince Henry;[32] it has even been read as a *roman à clef* of international politics, with Arcite as Henry, who has to die before his sister Elizabeth (Emilia) can marry her betrothed Frederick (Palamon).[33] In *The Two Noble Kinsmen*, the elements are similar to Chaucer's, but their treatment is noticeably different, and the end result unsettling: as Philip Finkelpearl has written, '[a]lthough the knightly code may originally have been designed to curb uncivilized instincts, here it sanctions and dignifies the urge of revenge, murder, and suicide'.[34]

Richard Hillman sees the fundamental contradictions as suggestive of an unbridgeable gap between medieval and Jacobean notions of chivalry:

'[p]recisely by endlessly trying and failing to measure up to the inherited images of romance perfection, these pale Jacobean imitations deconstruct the very business of image-making. They are trapped by their own attempted appropriation of a medieval past'.[35] The kinsmen's 'failure to measure up' is, moreover, treated harshly, even callously. The chivalric contest now carries a death penalty for the loser, and there is virtually no time lost between the winner's death and the loser's marriage. The death of one knight, an incidental detail in Chaucer (since it does not matter who marries the lady), here becomes essential to the happy ending. Significantly, a successful conclusion can only come at what Palamon calls the 'miserable end of our alliance' (V, iv, 86), the accident in which Arcite is fatally injured. Even here, the nature of his death—Arcite is left hanging upside down from his mount, after the horse rears away from a spark from the cobbles ('Arcite's legs, being higher than his head, / Seemed with strange art to hang' (V, iv, 78–9))—suggests something less than chivalric. As Richard Abrams notes, '[b]y the play's end, disabused of *The Knight's Tale*'s heroic mystique, we recognise the strangeness of a world where a question of love-rights is automatically referred to a determination of which kinsman is the stronger fighter'.[36]

Arcite must die for Palamon to win: as Palamon laments, 'That we should things desire, which do cost us / The loss of our desire! That nought could buy / Dear love, but loss of dear love' (V, iv, 110–12). *The Two Noble Kinsmen* demonstrates, and demands, highly developed understanding of concepts of friendship and kinship, developed enough to accommodate both parody and sincerity about such concepts. The friendship of Palamon and Arcite is no more than a game to while away long hours of incarceration; their constantly reiterated claims to kinship dissolve in the face of a prize (Emilia) that might benefit them as individuals and their immediate family groups; the play's happy ending necessitates the dissolution of their 'alliance'. Fletcher and Shakespeare indulge their audience in the comfortable humanist myth of *amicitia*, and the reliable codes of chivalric courtship, only to force that audience to accept the fact that ultimately these are no more than myths and codes, and that they cannot thrive together. We are faced with the sobering fact that artistic closure is not always compatible with social reality: to secure our desired happy ending, there may be fatalities.

Notes

1. For the limited critical bibliography to 1990 see Proudfoot, *'Henry VIII'*, pp. 391–2. The only monograph devoted to the play is Bertram, *Shakespeare and 'The Two Noble Kinsmen'*.

2. Thompson, *Shakespeare's Chaucer*, p. 166.

3. Donaldson, *The Swan at the Well*, p. 50.

4. Spencer, 'The Two Noble Kinsmen', p. 256.

5. Wickham, 'The Two Noble Kinsmen', p. 168.

6. See The Two Noble Kinsmen, ed. Potter, 'Introduction', pp. 2–6.

7. Spencer, 'The Two Noble Kinsmen', p. 255. See also The Two Noble Kinsmen, ed. Potter, pp. 24–34. The 'collaboration' argument is also used to explain away the problematic Jailer's Daughter subplot, but my focus here is on the Palamon and Arcite story.

8. Waith, 'Shakespeare and Fletcher', pp. 239–42; Hillman, 'Shakespeare's romantic innocents', p. 73.

9. Hillman, 'Shakespeare's romantic innocents', pp. 70, 71.

10. The classic survey of male friendship in Renaissance English literature remains Mills, One Soul in Bodies Twain.

11. For a discussion of this genre see Miller, Stages of Desire, Ch. 5.

12. See Elyot, Boke Named the Gouernour (1531); for the importance of this story, see Hutson, The Usurer's Daughter, Ch. 2.

13. Spencer, 'The Two Noble Kinsmen', p. 270.

14. Waith, 'Shakespeare and Fletcher', p. 236.

15. The importance of kinship rather than friendship in The Two Noble Kinsmen is stressed in Mills, One Soul in Bodies Twain, pp. 322–3, but he does not address the particular nature of this kinship.

16. Rubin, 'The traffic in women'; Sedgwick, Between Men.

17. Klapisch-Zuber, Women, Family, and Ritual, pp. 117–18.

18. Wrightson, English Society, pp. 44–51, p. 47.

19. Fletcher, A County Community, p. 48.

20. James, Society, Politics and Culture, p. 325.

21. For other uses of 'cousin' and 'coz' see II, ii, 4; II, ii, 63; II, ii, 96; II, ii, 107; II, ii 126; II, ii, 131; III, i, 43; III, i, 69; III, iii, 1; III, iii, 20; III, iii, 23; III, vi, 1; III, vi, 44; III, vi, 47; III, vi, 53; III, vi, 61; III, vi, 73; III, vi, 82; III, vi, 117; III, vi, 262; III, vi, 299; V, i, 23; V, i, 31; V, iv, 93; V, iv, 109.

22. Similarly, 'cousinage' can refer to the writ whereby a legal claim for land is made by one claiming to be a cousin to the deceased.

23. Fletcher, A County Community, p. 48.

24. References are to The Riverside Chaucer.

25. See Jardine and Stewart, Hostage to Fortune.

26. See Anthony Standen to Anthony Bacon, 3 February 1593/4, Lambeth Palace Library MS 650, fols 80–2 (art. 50). This incident is discussed at greater length in Jardine and Stewart, Hostage to Fortune, pp. 11–17.

27. Masten, Textual Intercourse, p. 49.

28. Bate, Shakespeare and Ovid, p. 265.

29. See Saslow, Ganymede in the Renaissance; Barkan, Transuming Passions; Smith, Homosexual Desire, Ch. 3.

30. Golding, The XV Bookes (1603), sig. Q8^v (Book X, ll. 155–61).

31. For Pelops, see Golding, The XV Bookes, sig. K8^v (Book VI, ll. 515–25).

32. See for example Hillman, 'Shakespeare's romantic innocents', p. 79; Finkelpearl, 'Two distincts, division none', pp. 184–99.

33. Wickham, 'The Two Noble Kinsmen', passim.

34. Finkelpearl, 'Two distincts, division none', p. 191.

35. Hillman, 'Shakespeare's romantic innocents', p. 71.

36. Abrams, 'Gender confusion', p. 75.

BIBLIOGRAPHY

Abrams, Richard, "Gender Confusion and Sexual Politics in *The Two Noble Kinsmen*," in *Drama, Sex and Politics, Themes in Drama 7*, ed. James Redmond (Cambridge: Cambridge University Press, 1985), pp. 69–76

Bate, Jonathan, *Shakespeare and Ovid* (Oxford: Clarendon Press, 1993)

Bertram, Paul, *Shakespeare and "The Two Noble Kinsmen"* (New Brunswick, N.J.: Rutgers University Press, 1965)

Chaucer, Geoffrey, *The Riverside Chaucer*, ed. F. N. Robinson, gen. ed. Larry D. Benson (Oxford: Oxford University Press, 1987, 3rd edn)

Donaldson, E. Talbot, *The Swan at the Well: Shakespeare Reading Chaucer* (New Haven: Yale University Press, 1985)

Elyot, Thomas, *Boke Names the Gouernour* (London, 1531)

Finkelpearl, Philip J. "Two Distincts, Division None: Shakespeare and Fletcher's *The Two Noble Kinsmen* of 1613," in *Elizabethan Theater: Essays in Honor of S. Schoenbaum*, eds. R. B. Parker and S. P. Zitner (Newark: University of Delaware Press, 1996), pp. 184–99

Fletcher, Anthony, *A Country Community in Peace and War: Sussex 1600–1660* (London: Longman, 1975)

Golding, Arthur, trans. *The XV Bookes of P. Ouidius Naso, Entituled Metamorphosis* (London, 1603)

Hillman, Richard, "Shakespeare's Romantic Innocents and the Misappropriation of the Romance Past: The Case of *The Two Noble Kinsmen*," *Shakespeare Survey*, 43 (1991): 69–89

Hutson, Lorna, *The Usurer's Daughter: Male Friendship and Fictions of Women in Sixteenth-Century England* (London and New York: Routledge, 1994)

James, Mervyn, *Society, Politics and Culture: Studies in Early Modern England* (Cambridge: Cambridge University Press, 1986)

Jardine, Lisa, and Alan Stewart, *Hostage to Fortune: The Troubled Life of Francis Bacon 1561–1626* (London: Gollancz, 1998)

Klapisch-Zuber, Christiane, *Women, Family, and Ritual in Renaissance Italy*, trans. Lydia Cochrane (Chicago and London: University of Chicago Press, 1985)

Masten, Jeffrey, *Textual Intercourse: Collaboration, Authorship, and Sexualities in Renaissance Drama* (Cambridge: Cambridge University Press, 1997)

Miller, Carl, *Stages of Desire: Gay Theatre's Hidden History* (London: Cassell, 1996)

Mill, Lauren J., *One Soul in Bodies Twain: Friendship in Tudor Literature and Tudor Drama* (Bloomingtom, Ind.: Principia Press, 1937)

Proudfoot, G. R., "*Henry VIII (All Is True), The Two Noble Kinsmen*, and the Apocryphal Plays," in *Shakespeare: A Bibliographical Guide*, ed. Stanley Wells (Oxford: Oxford University Press, 1990), pp. 381–403

Rubin, Gayle, "The Traffic in Women: Notes on a 'Political Economy' of Sex," in *Towards an Anthropology of Women*, ed. Rayna Reiter (New York: Monthly Review Press, 1975)

Saslow, James M., *Ganymede in the Renaissance: Homosexuality in Art and Society* (New Haven: Yale University Press, 1986)

Sedgwick, Eve Kosofsky, *Between Men: English Literature and Male Homosocial Desire* (New York: Columbia University Press, 1985)

Shakespeare, William, and John Fletcher, *The Two Noble Kinsmen*, ed. L. D. Potter (London: Routledge, 1997)

Spencer, Theodore, "*The Two Noble Kinsmen*," *Modern Philology*, 36 (1938–9), 255–76

Thompson, Ann, *Shakespeare's Chaucer: A Study in Literary Origins* (Liverpool: Liverpool University Press, 1978)

Waith, Eugene M. "Shakespeare and Fletcher on Love and Friendship," *Shakespeare Studies*, 18 (1986), 235–50

Wickham, Glynne, "The Two Noble Kinsmen or A Midsummer Night's Dream, Part II?," in *The Elizabethan Theatre VII: Papers Given at the Seventh International Conference on Elizabethan Theatre Held at the University of Waterloo, Ontario, in July 1997*, ed. G. R. Hibbard (London and Basingstoke: Macmillan, 1980), pp. 167–96

Wrightson, Keith, *English Society 1580–1680* (London: Hutchinson, 1982)

W.H. AUDEN

Troilus and Cressida

In considering *Troilus and Cressida*, *All's Well That Ends Well*, and *Measure for Measure*, not wholly successful plays, the first thing that comes to mind is the difference between a major and a minor writer—which is not necessarily the difference between better and worse. We can forget the bad writers. The minor artist, who can be idiosyncratic, keeps to one thing, does it well, and keeps on doing it—Thomas Campion, for example, A. E. Housman, and in music, Claude Debussy. There are minor writers who can mean more to us than any major writer, because their worlds are closest to ours. Great works of art can be hard to read—in a sense, boring to read. Whom do I read with the utmost pleasure? Not Dante, to my mind the greatest of poets, but Ronald Firbank. The minor writer never risks failure. When he discovers his particular style and vision, his artistic history is over.

The major writer, on the other hand, is of two kinds. One is the kind who spends most of his life preparing to produce a masterpiece, like Dante or Proust. Such writers have a long history in developing their writing, and they risk dying before it bears fruit. The other kind of major artist is engaged in perpetual endeavors. The moment such an artist learns to do something, he stops and tries to do something else, something new—like Shakespeare, or Wagner, or Picasso. How do the two different types of major writers create their work, and what is important to them? The first type is interested in

From *Lectures on Shakespeare*, reconstructed and edited by Arthur Kirsch, pp. 166–80, 381–82. Copyright © 2000 by Arthur Kirsch for the notes and © 2000 by the estate of W.H. Auden for lectures and writings by Auden.

103

finding out what the masterpiece will be, the second is more interested in discovering how to tackle a new problem and is not concerned about whether the work will succeed. Shakespeare is always prepared to risk failure. *Troilus and Cressida*, *Measure for Measure* and *All's Well That Ends Well* don't quite come off, whereas almost every poem of Housman does. But if we don't understand these plays, we won't understand the great tragedies.

What are Shakespeare's problems in *Troilus and Cressida*? First, the technical ones: he must perfect a style to deal with matter he has not previously dealt with. Second, he must decide what, in his material, is interesting and important. Initially, as we saw in *Hamlet*, there is the problem of vocabulary, particularly the use of a Latinized vocabulary—in *Troilus and Cressida*, words such as "vindicative" (IV.v.107), "tortive," "errant" (I.iii.9), and "prenominate" (IV.v.250). There are also many double nouns and adjectives in *Henry V*, *Hamlet*, and *Troilus and Cressida*—"in the fan and wind of your fair sword" (V.iii.41) or "ridiculous and awkward action" (I.iii.149), for example, in *Troilus and Cressida*—that result in a very elaborate and involved style of speech. Metaphors are developed elaborately to illustrate thought, in contrast with Julius Caesar, for example, where they are decorative.

Shakespeare inherited two kinds of style. The first was the passionate choleric style, inherited from Marlowe, that is found in Talbot's speeches in *Henry VI*. Ajax's speech to the trumpeter is an example in *Troilus and Cressida*:

> Now crack thy lungs and split thy brazen pipe.
> Blow, villain, till thy sphered bias cheek
> Outswell the colic of puff'd Aquilon.
> Come, stretch thy chest and let thy eyes spout blood.
>   (IV.v.7–10)

The other style Shakespeare inherited was the affective, antithetically balanced style of lyric and reflective character that we find in *The Rape of Lucrece*:

> "Time's glory is to calm contending kings,
> To unmask falsehood and bring truth to light,
> To stamp the seal of time in aged things,
> To wake the morn and sentinel the night,
> To wrong the wronger till he render right,
>   To ruinate proud buildings with thy hours,
>   And smear with dust their glitt'ring golden tow'rs;
> "To fill with wormholes stately monuments,

To feed oblivion with decay of things,
To blot old books and alter their contents,
To pluck the quills from ancient ravens' wings,
To dry the old oak's sap and cherish springs,
  To spoil antiquities of hammer'd steel
  And turn the giddy round of Fortune's wheel;
"To show the beldame daughters of her daughter,
To make the child a man, the man a child,
To slay the tiger that cloth live by slaughter,
To tame the unicorn and lion wild,
To mock the subtle in themselves beguil'd,
  To cheer the ploughman with increaseful crops
  And waste huge stones with little water-drops.
   (939–59)

In *Troilus and Cressida*, by contrast, Shakespeare is developing the kind of reflective and intellectual style we see in Ulysses' speech to Achilles on Time:

Time hath, my lord, a wallet at his back,
Wherein he puts alms for oblivion,
A great-siz'd monster of ingratitudes.
Those scraps are good deeds past, which are devour'd
As fast as they are made, forgot as soon
As done. Perseverance, dear my lord,
Keeps honour bright. To have done is to hang
Quite out of fashion, like a rusty mail
In monumental mock'ry. Take the instant way;
For honour travels in a strait so narrow
Where one but goes abreast. Keep then the path,
For emulation hath a thousand sons
That one by one pursue. If you give way,
Or hedge aside from the direct forthright,
Like to an ent'red tide they all rush by
And leave you hindmost;
Or, like a gallant horse fall'n in first rank,
Lie there for pavement to the abject rear,
O'errun and trampled on. Then what they do in present,
Though less than yours in past, must o'ertop yours;
For Time is like a fashionable host,
That slightly shakes his parting guest by th' hand,

And with his arms outstretch'd as he would fly
Grasps in the comer. The welcome ever smiles,
And farewell goes out sighing. Let not virtue seek
Remuneration for the thing it was!
    (III.iii.145–70)

This is a style of reflection in a specific situation, calculated for a particular
effect: Ulysses is trying, with intellectual argument, to get Achilles to act.
Shakespeare had previously represented this kind of argument in prose.

    Parallel to this verse, Shakespeare is developing something new in
prose, a kind of violent prose that reaches its full flower in the speeches of
the Fool in *King Lear*. We see it in Thersites' diatribe against Agamemnon
and Menelaus:

> With too much blood and too little brain these two may run mad;
> but if with too much brain and too little blood they do, I'll be a
> curer of madmen. Here's Agamemnon, an honest fellow enough
> and one that loves quails, but he has not so much brain as earwax;
> and the goodly transformation of Jupiter there, his brother, the bull,
> the primitive statue and oblique memorial of cuckolds, a thrifty
> shoeing horn in a chain, hanging at his brother's leg—to what form
> but that he is should wit larded with malice, and malice forced with
> wit, turn him to? To an ass were nothing: he is both ass and ox: to
> an ox were nothing; he is both ox and ass. To be a dog, a mule, a cat,
> a fitchook, a toad, a lizard, an owl, a puttock, or a herring without a
> roe, I would not care; but to be Menelaus, I would conspire against
> destiny. Ask me not what I would be if I were not Thersites; for I
> care not to be the louse of a lazar, so I were not Menelaus—Hoy-
> day! sprites and fires!
>
>   (V.i.53–73)

    Hamlet uses verse for great emotions in *Hamlet*, and prose for ordinary
relations. In the opening scene of *Troilus and Cressida*, Troilus speaks in verse
and Pandarus in prose, and in the next scene Pandarus and Cressida speak in
prose to each other, and Cressida speaks in verse when she is alone. The third
scene, the Greek council scene, is entirely in verse. In the first scene of Act II,
Ajax and Thersites speak to each other in prose, in the next, the Trojan council
scene, there is only poetry, and in the third scene, in the Greek camp, the men
talk in prose to Thersites and largely in verse to each other. The beginning and
the end of the orchard scene (III.ii) are in verse, otherwise Troilus and Cressida's wooing is in prose, except at its emotional height. Pandarus, Thersites,

and other detached characters always talk in prose. Troilus, Cressida, and others, when they know what their relation is—warrior, lover—use poetry, and when they are uncertain or indifferent, as in the scene of Pandarus, Helen, and Paris together (III.i), they use prose.

The matter of the play is: (a) the Homeric story of the Trojan War, the archetype of male heroism, with its accompanying issues of courage, honor, comradeship in arms, and (b) the love story of Troilus and Cressida, the great medieval archetype of courtly love. The conventions of both stories, one of tragic heroism, the other of pathetic love, are transformed in the play. In what does the tragedy of Homer consist? What happens is really ordained by the gods, and human emotion is juxtaposed against the indifference of everlasting nature. In the foreground are men locked in battle, killing and being killed, farther off their wives, children, and servants waiting anxiously for the outcome, overhead, watching the spectacle with interest and at times interfering, the gods who know neither sorrow nor death, and around them all indifferent and unchanging, the natural world of sky and sea and earth. Though Castor and Pollux are dead, the life-giving earth is our mother still. The same sense of how things are, how they always have been, and always will be, is conveyed in *Beowulf* in the final dirge for Beowulf, and in Achilles' dialogue with old Priam at the end of the *Iliad*: "Neither may I tend [my father] as he groweth old, since very far from my country I am dwelling in Troy-land, to vex thee and thy children." Life makes no sense, but the moment of heroism, the moment of loyalty, does. "Hige sceal þe heardra, / heorte þe cenre, / mod sceal þe mare / þe ure maegen lytlað," Byrhtwold says to his expiring warriors in *The Battle of Maldon*. "Mind must be the resoluter, / heart the bolder, / courage must be the greater, / as our strength dwindles."

In *Troilus and Cressida* the characters are not driven by a fate from which they cannot escape. They know what they are doing and don't believe in it. Troilus says of the war, at the very beginning of the play,

> Peace, you ungracious clamours! peace, rude sounds!
> Fools on both sides, Helen must needs be fair
> When with your blood you daily paint her thus!
> I cannot fight upon this argument;
> It is too starv'd a subject for my sword.
>   (I.i.92–96)

Hector and Troilus are the only two characters in the play with the faintest pretense of nobility. In the Trojan council scene, Hector argues that reason demands Helen should be given up, and Troilus that honor demands she should be kept:

> *Hect.* Brother, she is not worth what she doth cost
> The holding.
> *Tro.* What is aught but as 'tis valu'd?
> *Hect.* But value dwells not in particular will:
> It holds his estimate and dignity
> As well wherein 'tis precious of itself
> As in the prizer. 'Tis mad idolatry
> To make the service greater than the god;
> And the will dotes that is attributive
> To what infectiously itself affects
> Without some image of th' affected merit. . . .
> Or, is your blood
> So madly hot that no discourse of reason,
> Nor fear of bad success in a bad cause,
> Can qualify the same?
>   (II.ii.51–60, 115–18)

Hector continues to chide the Trojans for perpetuating wrong by doing more wrong, but then suddenly and lamely agrees with Troilus' appeal to honor:

>   Thus to persist
> In doing wrong extenuates not wrong,
> But makes it much more heavy. Hector's opinion
> Is this in way of truth. Yet ne'ertheless,
> My sprightly brethren, I propend to you
> In resolution to keep Helen still;
> For 'tis a cause that hath no mean dependence
> Upon our joint and several dignities.
>   (II.ii.186–93)

The Homeric hero finds himself in a tragic situation from which there is no escape. Shakespeare's people, for the sake of glory, refuse to escape when escape is possible. Diomedes tells Paris quite plainly that Helen is worthless and that both he and Menelaus are fools for fighting over her:

>   Both alike.
> He merits well to have her that doth seek her,
> Not making any scruple of her soilure,
> With such a hell of pain and world of charge;
> And you as well to keep her, that defend her,
> Not palating the taste of her dishonour,

With such a costly loss of wealth and friends.
He like a puling cuckold would drink up
The lees and dregs of a flat tamed piece;
You, like a lecher, out of whorish loins
Are pleas'd to breed out your inheritors.
Both merits pois'd; each weighs nor less nor more;
But he as he, the heavier for a whore.
Par. You are too bitter to your countrywoman.
Dio. She's bitter to her country. Hear me, Paris:
For every false drop in her bawdy veins
A Grecian's life hath sunk; for every scruple
Of her contaminated carrion weight
A Troyan hath been slain. Since she could speak
She hath not given so many good words breath
As for her Greeks and Troyans suff'red death.

Paris answers, cynically,

Fair Diomed, you do as chapmen do,
Dispraise the thing that you desire to buy;
But we in silence hold this virtue well,
We'll not commend what we intend to sell.
    (IV.i.54–78)

In many other ways as well, the play doesn't conform to heroic convention. Achilles gets a letter from Hecuba with a token from her daughter, his "fair love" (V.i.45), and he refuses to fight. He forgets his cause, so there is no tragic conflict, as in heroic tragedy. When he remembers it after Patroclus is killed, he takes the extremely unheroic line of butchering the unarmed Hector:

Achil. Look, Hector, how the sun begins to set;
How ugly night comes breathing at his heels.
Even with the vail and dark'ning of the sun,
To close the day up, Hector's life is done.
Hect. I am unarm'd; forgo this vantage, Greek.
Achil. Strike, fellows, strike! This is the man I seek.
    [*Hector falls.*]
    (V.viii.5–10)

Ajax and Achilles have no loyalty, they are interested only in themselves. The other comradeship in arms, the relationship of Achilles and

Patroclus—compare the biblical story of David and Jonathan—is reduced to sexual love. Patroclus admits he has little stomach for the wars. His biggest thing is his ability to amuse Achilles with imitations. The characters are like the grubby little boys from Steig cartoons, except that they know what they're doing and people get killed.

Aeneas and Diomedes, when they greet each other in Troy, are courteous, but also defiant and savage:

> *Aene.* Health to you, valiant sir,
> During all question of the gentle truce;
> But when I meet you arm'd, as black defiance
> As heart can think or courage execute!
> *Dio.* The one and other Diomed embraces.
> Our bloods are now in calm, and so long, health!
> But when contention and occasion meet,
> By Jove, I'll play the hunter for thy life
> With all my force, pursuit, and policy.
> *Aene.* And thou shalt hunt a lion that will fly
> With his face backward. In humane gentleness
> Welcome to Troy! now by Anchises' life,
> Welcome indeed! By Venus' hand I swear,
> No man alive can love in such a sort
> The thing he means to kill more excellently.
> *Dio.* We sympathize. Jove let Aeneas live,
> If to my sword his fate be not the glory,
> A thousand complete courses of the sun!
> But in mine emulous honour let him die,
> With every joint a wound, and that to-morrow!
> (IV.i.10–29)

Directions to the stage director of *Troilus and Cressida*: everything should be made grotesque, the characters presented as caricatures in the Dickens tradition. Agamemnon, Menelaus, Achilles, Ajax, must be enormous. Nestor must be a tiny, incredibly drivelling old man, Patroclus a 52nd Street queen, Helen an expensive whore, like the Second Mrs. Tanqueray, and Cressida like Mildred in *Of Human Bondage*. Pandarus must be fat and plainly syphilitic.

The story of Troilus and Cressida draws upon a tradition including Dares, Boccaccio, Chaucer, and Henryson. In Chaucer, Criseyde doesn't yield to Troilus until midway in the third book, the fourth book treats their love, and the fifth is about her betrayal. In Shakespeare there is no wooing. First, Cressida likes Troilus, second, they go to bed, and third, she betrays him very soon after. C. S. Lewis sees Chaucer's Criseyde as "a woman who in a chaste society would certainly have lived a chaste widow." But if, Lewis says, in the society and circumstances in which she does live,

> she yields, she commits no sin against the social code of her age and country: she commits no unpardonable sin against any code I know of—unless, perhaps, against that of the Hindus. By Christian standards, forgivable: by the rules of courtly love, needing no forgiveness: this is all that need be said of Cryseide's act in granting the Rose to Troilus. But her betrayal of him is not so easily dismissed.
>
> Here there is, of course, no question of acquittal. "False Cryseide" she has been ever since the story was first told, and will be till the end. And her offence is rank. By the code of courtly love it is unpardonable; in Christian ethics it is as far below her original unchastity as Brutus and Iscariot, in Dante's hell, lie lower than Paolo and Francesca. But we must not misunderstand her sin; we must not so interpret it as to cast any doubt upon the sincerity of her first love.

Lewis goes on to say that if we ask how this sincerity "is compatible with her subsequent treachery," the answer is a further consideration of her character:

> Chaucer has so emphasized the ruling passion of his heroine, that we cannot mistake it. It is Fear—fear of loneliness, of old age, of death, of love, and of hostility; of everything, indeed, that can be feared. And from this Fear springs the only positive passion which can be permanent in such a nature; the pitiable longing, more childlike than womanly, for protection. . . . . What cruelty it is, to subject such a woman to the test of absence—and of absence with no assured future of reunion, absence compelled by the terrible outer-world of law and politics and force (which she cannot face), absence amid alien scenes and voices.

> With wommen fewe, among the Grekes stronge.

Every one can foresee the result.

Once she is in Greek hands, Lewis writes,

> Diomede becomes, no longer the alternative to Troilus, but the alternative to flight. The picture of herself in Diomede's arms gains the all but irresistible attraction that it blots out the unbearable

picture of herself stealing out past the sentries in the darkness. And so, weeping and half-unwilling, and self-excusing, and repentant by anticipation before her guilt is consummated, the unhappy creature becomes the mistress of her Greek lover, grasping at the last chance of self-respect with the words

> To Diomede algate I wol be trewe.

Shakespeare's Cressida, on the other hand, wants power and can play hard to get:

> Yet hold I off. Women are angels, wooing:
> Things won are done; joy's soul lies in the doing.
> That she belov'd knows naught that knows not this:
> Men prize the thing ungain'd more than it is.
> That she was never yet that ever knew
> Love got so sweet as when desire did sue.
> Therefore this maxim out of love I teach:
> Achievement is command; ungain'd, beseech.
> Then, though my heart's content firm love doth bear,
> Nothing of that shall from mine eyes appear.
>   (I.ii.312–21)

The first conversation between Troilus and Cressida is coarse and sexual.

> *Tro.* O, let my lady apprehend no fear! In all Cupid's pageant
> there is presented no monster.
> *Cres.* Nor nothing monstrous neither?
> *Tro.* Nothing but our undertakings when we vow to weep seas,
> live in fire, eat rocks, tame tigers—thinking it harder for our
> mistress to devise imposition enough than for us to undergo any
> difficulty imposed. This is the monstruosity in love, lady, that
> the will is infinite and the execution confin'd, that the desire is
> boundless and the act a slave to limit.
> *Cres.* They say all lovers swear more performance than they are
> able, and yet reserve an ability that they never perform, vowing
> more than the perfection of ten, and discharging less than the
> tenth part of one. They that have the voice of lions and the acts of
> hares, are they not monsters?
>   (III.ii.79–96)

Ulysses ticks Cressida off at once:

Fie, fie upon her!
There's language in her eye, her cheek, her lip;
Nay, her foot speaks. Her wanton spirits look out
At every joint and motive of her body.
O, these encounterers so glib of tongue,
That give accosting welcome ere it comes
And wide unclasp the tables of their thoughts
To every ticklish reader—set them down
For sluttish spoils of opportunity
And daughters of the game!
    (IV.v.54–63)

She's sunk when she attempts to deal with Diomedes. His interest is entirely physical, and he has a better trick than she has. He does what she did with Troilus: he threatens to leave her. At the end she gives him Troilus' sleeve, saying that it belonged to one "that lov'd me better than you will" (V.ii.89–90).

Pandarus is reduced from the interesting, complicated servant of *Amour* we find in Chaucer to an old syphilitic man depending upon second-hand pleasures. The only pleasure that his own impotence allows him is the voyeuristic encouragement of others, like the Earl of Rochester's maimed debauchee:

Thus, Statesman-like I'll saucily impose,
    And, safe from danger, valiantly advise;
Shelter'd in Impotence urge you to Blows,
    And, being good for nothing else, be wise.

Pandarus is loyal both to Troilus and courtly love in Chaucer, he is loyal just to pandering in Shakespeare.

Troilus is supposed to be fairly nice by comparison to Pandarus and Cressida, but not if we look closely. Compare the speech in which Juliet looks forward to her night with Romeo with the speech in which Troilus anticipates sleeping with Cressida. Juliet's speech, "Come, civil night," in which she anticipates the loss of her maidenhead and the consummation of her marriage, is frankly sexual—"O, I have bought the mansion of a love, / But not possess'd it" (III.ii.26–27), but it is the speech of someone thinking of a particular person:

Come, night; come, Romeo; come thou day in night;
For thou wilt lie upon the wings of night
Whiter than new snow upon a raven's back.

Come, gentle night; come, loving, black-brow'd night;
Give me my Romeo.
    (III.ii.17–21)

Troilus says, in expectation of Cressida's coming,

I am giddy; expectation whirls me round.
Th' imaginary relish is so sweet
That it enchants my sense. What will it be
When that the wat'ry palates taste indeed
Love's thrice-repured nectar? Death, I fear me;
Sounding destruction; or some joy too fine,
Too subtile-potent, tun'd too sharp in sweetness
For the capacity of my ruder powers.
I fear it much; and I do fear besides
That I shall lose distinction in my joys,
As doth a battle when they charge on heaps
The enemy flying.
    (III.ii.19–30)

Troilus's reverie is a marvellous analysis of a particular experience, but it is
quite independent of the person with whom he is going to sleep. Chaucer's
Troilus is kind and chivalrous—"the smale bestes leet he gon biside." Shakespeare's Troilus is not. He is "more dangerous" than Hector, Ulysses says,

For Hector in his blaze of wrath subscribes
To tender objects, but he in heat of action
Is more vindicative than jealous love.
    (IV.v.105–7)

Troilus makes his nature clear in telling Hector,

Brother, you have a vice of mercy in you
Which better fits a lion than a man. . . . . .
  For th' love of all the gods,
Let's leave the hermit Pity with our mother;
And when we have our armours buckled on,
The venomed vengeance ride upon our swords,
Spur them to ruthful work, rein them from ruth!
  Hect. Fie, savage, fie!
    (V.iii.37–38, 44–49)

Troilus and Cressida is not a satire merely. There are two kinds of satire. There is a satire of sacred abuse, whose purpose is to produce a catharsis of resentment, a holiday from conventions designed to keep the conventions solid. The second kind exposes abuses, and even attacks the so-called norm in order to establish a new norm. But the very idea of a norm is attacked in Shakespeare's *Troilus and Cressida.* There is no universal in the play. In *Hamlet,* where the ego and the self are separate, the self becomes questionable, and this separation means an awareness of, and a responsibility for, the self. The process is not reversible. Once it's experienced, it is very hard to think back to your prior state. One can imagine people different from oneself, but it is difficult to imagine a person with less degree of consciousness than oneself. We write about others as if they were aware of what we see to be their rationalizations. What makes *Troilus and Cressida* unsatisfactory and at the same time so malign is that the characters behave with awareness in a way that aware characters would not behave. Hamlet tries to free his self by freeing it of all relations, all the ties to society that determined his nature, but he is also afraid of losing himself. The next stage is the detached, observing ego—which differs from Brutus's *ataraxia* because Brutus is unaware of his nature. An aware person recognizes the lack of freedom of feeling, but his awareness gives him the freedom of analysis and an aversion to emotional display in which only honest emotion is admissible. Hamlet's detachment works backwards into emotion.

The characters in *Troilus and Cressida* have an extraordinary verbosity. Words are vehicles of detachment, a means to *ataraxia*, as Robert Graves points out:

Children are dumb to say how hot the day is,
How hot the scent is of the summer rose,
How dreadful the black wastes of evening sky,
How dreadful the tall soldiers drumming by.
But we have speech, that cools the hottest sun,
And speech that dulls the hottest rose's scent.
We spell away the overhanging night,
We spell away the soldiers and the fright.
There's a cool web of language winds us in,
Retreat from too much gladness, too much fear:
We grow sea-green at last and coldly die
In brininess and volubility.
But if we let our tongues lose self-possession,
Throwing off language and its wateriness
Before our death, instead of when death comes,

Facing the brightness of the children's day,
Facing the rose, the dark sky and the drums,
We shall go mad no doubt and die that way.

Thersites says, when he refuses to fight Margarelon the Bastard,

I am a bastard too; I love bastards. I am bastard begot, bastard instructed, bastard in mind, bastard in valour, in everything illegitimate. One bear will not bite another, and wherefore should one bastard? Take heed, the quarrel's most ominous to us. If the son of a whore fight for a whore, he tempts judgment. Farewell, bastard.

(V.vii.16–23)

If we compare this speech to Falstaff's soliloquy on honor, we see that Falstaff is arguing for straight self-preservation, Thersites for ego preservation. It is a triumph of the ego to be honest about the self. Shakespeare works through this process in the plays of this period in a way that reveals, in the tragedies, how pride differs from hybris. In classical tragedy, man thinks his self to be more secure than it is. In Shakespearean tragedy, pride begins with the desire to be a god, a desire to escape from one's finiteness. One tries to hide this finiteness by power over others, like Macbeth, or by the idolatry of the individual in the romantic tradition, or by the idolatry of convention in law, of the infinite We in which the individual is annihilated. In the great tragedies the knowledge of what they are doing is hidden from the heroes, and a really mad world is created by the hero with a dynamic mania. In *Troilus and Cressida*, where the characters are and remain maniacs and are aware of it, we get the feeling that this is the world, not *a* world. Only by reading plays like this can we see how terrifying *Othello* and *Macbeth* really are.

Once there is a revelation of what's going on, there is either destruction or a new relationship. A man who hasn't questioned the value of his own existence or of any social effort is still a child. As Martin Buber explains, it is only at that point that man achieves individual history. Beasts of prey can have a biography and even state annals, but only man can have history, by having responsibility. In order to reach that point of responsibility, to be related to truth, one must see truth as over against the self. That is why all progress depends upon the experience in which life and one's nature are called into question. As G. K. Chesterton writes in "The Sword of Surprise,"

Sunder me from my bones, O sword of God,
Till they stand stark and strange as do the trees;
That I whose heart goes up with the soaring woods

May marvel as much at these.
Sunder me from my blood that in the dark
I hear that red ancestral river run,
Like branching buried floods that find the sea
But never see the sun.
Give me miraculous eyes to see my eyes,
Those rolling mirrors made alive in me,
Terrible crystal more incredible
Than all the things they see.
Sunder me from my soul, that I may see
The sins like streaming wounds, the life's brave beat;
Till I shall save myself, as I would save
A stranger in the street.

NOTES

This lecture has been reconstructed from notes by Ansen, Griffin, Lowenstein, and Bodenstein.

Page

103　Ronald Firbank (1886–1926). Auden wrote a review of Firbank for the *New York Times*, 20 November 1949, and an essay on his work for *The Listener*, 8 June 1961.

107　"In the foreground. . . . sea and earth.": From *FA*, 17.

107　"at the end of the Iliad": Homer, *Iliad*, Bk. 24, trans. Andrew Lang, Walter Leaf, Ernest Myers, *The Complete Works of Homer* (New York: Modern Library, 1935), 456.

107　*The Battle of Maldon*, ll. 312–13.

110　"biblical story of David and Jonathan": 1 Samuel.20.

110　"Steig cartoons": William Steig was a regular and extremely sardonic cartoonist for *The New Yorker*.

110　"Nestor . . . Patroclus . . . queen": a conflation of Bodenstein's and Ansen's notes. Bodenstein's notes say, "Nestor must be an old, tiny, dribbling 52nd Street Queen," Ansen's say, "Patroclus must be 52nd Street Queen." Cf. "September 1, 1939": "I sit in one of the dives / On Fifty-Second Street," and see Fuller, *Auden: A Commentary*, 290–91.

110　"the Second Mrs. Tanqueray": In Arthur Wing Pinero, *The Second Mrs. Tanqueray* (1893).

110　"like Mildred": In W. Somerset Maugham, *Of Human Bondage* (1915).

110　"Dares": Dares of Phrygia, reputed author of a lost pre-Homeric account of the Trojan War. A supposed Latin prose translation survives, *Daretis Phrygii de Excidio Trojae Historia* (5th century?), and was widely used by medieval authors.

110　Giovanni Boccaccio, *Il Filostrato* (ca. 1338).

110　Robert Henryson, *Testament of Cresseid* (1593).

111　"C. S. Lewis sees": *The Allegory of Love*, 183–89.

113 John Wilmot, Earl of Rochester, "The Maim'd Debauchee," *Collected Works of John Wilmot Earl of Rochester,* ed. John Hayward (London: Nonesuch Press, 1926).

114 "'the smale bestes. . . . '": Geoffrey Chaucer, *Troilus and Criseyde,* III. 1781.

115 Robert Graves, "The Cool Web," *Poems (1914–26)* (London: William Heinemann, 1928).

116 Martin Buber, *I and Thou* (1937), Part One.

116 G. K. Chesterton, "The Sword of Surprise," *The Collected Poems of G. K. Chesterton* (London: Cecil Palmer, 1927), 55.

RICHARD HARP

The Consolation of Romance:
Providence in Shakespeare's Late Plays

Know that the good are always powerful, and the evil always abject and weak, and that vices are not without punishment, nor virtue without reward, and that the good are always prosperous, and the evil unfortunate.

—Boethius, *The Consolation of Philosophy*, 4.1

I. Providence and the English Renaissance

"It is not too much to say," wrote Roy Battenhouse in 1941, "that the doctrine of Providence was the chief apologetic interest of Reformation times."[1] A more recent and more cautious assessment expands the terms of this generalization but still endorses the basic point: "The problems of predestination and foreknowledge, of providence and grace and of where freedom stands in relation to salvation were fiercely debated throughout the latter half of the sixteenth century."[2] In the Middle Ages the doctrine of fortune held immense sway in certain portrayals of life, such as Chaucer's *Monk's Tale*, but in Renaissance dramatic literature, and especially in Shakespeare's traditional four late romances—*Pericles*, *Cymbeline*, *The Winter's Tale*, and *The Tempest*—there was an emphasis on an individual's free cooperation with higher powers in forming his destiny. Which is not to say that such emphases were not also found in medieval moralities and romances such as the *Morte d'Arthur*, where knights "are 'happy' in the sense of fortunate when they are also 'happy' in the sense of virtuous and therefore filled with the

---

From *Shakespeare's Last Plays: Essays in Literature and Politics*, edited by Stephen W. Smith and Travis Curtright, pp. 17–34. Copyright © 2002 by Lexington Books.

119

grace of God."[3] In the Middle Ages, though, such sentiments could perhaps be taken for granted whereas for Shakespeare and his age, the inseparability of such themes as providence and authority "was a matter of moral faith," so much so that even a figure such as Gonzalo in *The Tempest*—not ineffectual, certainly, but far from powerful—may be considered, according to R. A. D. Grant, as a "direct human representative of the Providential power that lies behind the play."[4] And, although it is upon England that I will be concentrating here, this interest in God's mysterious ways was intense upon the Continent as well. Tragicomic plays, says Perry Gethner, "flourished in much of Europe in the early decades of the seventeenth century," and references in them to providence were common.[5] And finally, even up-to-date Continental theorists such as Pierre Gassendi (1592–1655), who sought to revive Epicureanism in the seventeenth century, still "disagreed with ancient atomists' materialistic and anti-providential outlook."[6]

While providence is a topic, then, that provoked extremely wide discussion in the Renaissance and is usually referred to at least in passing in any discussion of Shakespeare's romances, there has been little sustained investigation of it in relation to those plays. It is a subject somewhat like the letter in Poe's "The Purloined Letter," hidden in plain sight, so we shall here survey some of its features in *Pericles*, *Cymbeline*, *The Winter's Tale*, and *The Tempest*.

The great Roman philosopher Boethius is of fundamental importance in discussing questions of providence and its relation to such allied topics as destiny, fate, and free will. His influence upon medieval thought is a textbook commonplace but his prestige in the sixteenth century was also great. Antonio Poppi says his "eirenic approach and solutions were an influential legacy to [both] the Middle Ages and the Renaissance,"[7] as he softened the aversion of earlier church thinkers to the idea of fate by showing how it complemented the idea of providence. Fate or destiny (the two will be used synonymously here), was not, as for the Ancients, the supreme force of the universe but rather carried out in the temporal sphere the will of providence, which "is the very Divine reason itself, seated in the highest Prince, which disposeth all things. But Fate is a disposition inherent in changeable things, by which Providence connecteth all things in their due order."[8] Fate has at its disposal several agents to carry out the will of providence, some of which are similar to the instruments Shakespeare will employ in the plays: fate may accomplish its will "by the subordination of certain Divine spirits to Providence [Ariel in *The Tempest* is not divine but is obviously a spirit that works for the achievement of a greater good], or this fatal web [may] be woven by a soul or by the service of all nature or by the heavenly motion of the stars [innumerable examples in Shakespeare], by angelical virtue, or by diabolical industry, or by some or all of these" (4.6; 341–43). Providence is immovable and stable, while Fate in executing its service partakes of the changeableness of the things it directs.

The influence of Boethius only increased as the sixteenth century wore on, culminating in Queen Elizabeth's translation of *The Consolation of Philosophy* in 1593[9] and a further translation in 1609 (during the years Shakespeare was writing the romances), and the basic terms of his discussion were followed by a host of writers. Typically they saw providence's decrees being effected by Boethius' "the service of all nature." Richard Hooker, for instance, defines providence as the "natural generation and process of all things [that] receiveth order of proceeding from the settled stability of divine understanding."[10] He makes the same distinction as Boethius between providence and its minister destiny: "the things themselves here disposed by it, was wont by the ancient to be called natural Destiny. . . . Nature therefore is nothing else but God's instrument" (160). Or, as Milton defined the relationship in *Paradise Lost*, "God and Nature bid the same" (6.176). Graphically giving names to the manifestations of providence in the ancient world, Hooker says that "the heathens . . . gave him in the sky the name of Jupiter, in the air the name of Juno, in the water the name of Neptune, in the earth the name of Vesta and sometimes of Ceres, the name of Apollo in the sun . . . and to conclude, even so many guides of nature they dreamed of, as they saw there were kinds of things natural in the world" (160). Shakespeare of course still found many of these useful as agents of providential design in his romances, having Jupiter in *Cymbeline*, for example, foretell how suffering may lead to a good end, or using the Apollo of the Delphic Oracle to pronounce upon Hermione's innocence in *The Winter's Tale*, or including Juno and Ceres in the masque in *The Tempest* to help celebrate the fecundity of marriage. In general, I think, Shakespeare observes Boethius' distinction between providence and fate or destiny and is particularly skillful in picturing a great variety of natural agents (or "secondary causes," in the philosophers' terminology, as I will note below), mythological and human, which effect providential ends.

Other romantic literature of the period, of course, reflects providence as a central concern; Maurice Evans, for example, says that the most important theme of Sir Philip Sidney's *Arcadia* "is the mysterious but benevolent working of providence,"[11] but more secular-minded historians and essayists, such as Sir Walter Raleigh and Francis Bacon, also found an important place for providence in nature. Raleigh in his *History of the World* distinguishes between "prescience" and providence. Prescience is God's seeing the future and Raleigh makes the traditional distinction that such foreknowledge does not "impose any necessity or bind" the freedom of human beings, quoting Boethius in support. Providence, on the other hand, is "an intellectual knowledge"—called by the Greeks "pronoia"—which beholds past, present, and future and which "is the cause of their so being, which prescience (simply taken) is not."[12] Bacon says in his essay "Of Atheism" that when "the mind of man" looks upon the chain of secondary causes and "beholdeth the chain of them, confederate and linked together, it must needs fly to Providence and Deity."[13] And then, of course, poets and preachers such as John Donne and George Herbert continuously praise the providential design of the universe. "The world is a frame of so much harmony," Donne says in a sermon, that it must have had a workman, "for nothing can make it selfe." Furthermore, such a world God would not have turned over to fortune, and thus he sustains it "still by his watchfull Providence."[14] Donne, too, says that to foresee future actions is not to cause them (God foresees all things, even sins, "but yet his foresight is noe cause of them" [II, 152]), and he notes that "in corners where nothing sees us, God sees us, and in hell where wee shall see nothinge, he shall see us, too" (II, 150), a passage which might remind Shakespearians of the "duke of dark corners," Vincentio in *Measure for Measure* (4.3.157),[15] who doesn't exactly look into Hell but does spend time in a Viennese prison, a close enough approximation. And nearly all of Herbert's poetry is a paean to providence, none more so than his poem of that title, where he says that "sacred Providence" does "so strongly and so sweetly move, / While all things have their will, yet none but thine" (ll. 31–32),[16] a lyrical summary of Boethian doctrine.

If Boethius is the skeleton for this pervasive, indeed almost ubiquitous concern with providence in the sixteenth and seventeenth centuries, St. Thomas Aquinas provides much of the muscle and tissue. We are far removed from the times when the occasional scholar of a generation ago could find little influence of the "dumb ox" upon the period, although even today "It is sometimes forgotten that Aquinas reached his highest and widest measure of influence—among Protestants as well as Catholics—in the sixteenth and seventeenth centuries."[17] Thus we see even so occasional a philosophical scholar as Raleigh quoting Aquinas concerning the relation of fortune to providence: things may happen "besides the intention of the inferior, but not besides the intention of the superior."[18] St. Thomas's discussion of this matter included St. Augustine's comment that "Nothing happens at random in the world," which he illuminated in the course of his argument by saying that what appears to us as accidental is only so "compared to inferior causes, which, if compared to some higher cause, is directly intended." His example was of the "meeting of two servants in regard to themselves is by chance; but as compared to the master, who had ordered it, it is directly intended."[19]

II. Providence and Shakespeare's Villains:
The Turning of Evil to Good

Such distinctions are important in the world, and in Shakespeare's plays, not so much in the matter of accidental meetings of servants but rather in understanding how the evil deeds of men may lead to a good end, obviously crucial to any doctrine of providence. To prove that the universe is not governed by chance but by providence, it is necessary to show that things usually happen for the best; again Aquinas quotes St. Augustine: "Almighty God would in no wise permit evil to exist in His works, unless He were so almighty and so good as to produce good even from evil" (Pt. I, Q. 22, Art. 2), and the inequality and imperfection of things, St. Thomas adds, is the means whereby this divine wisdom is made manifest (Pt. I, Q. 47, Art. 2). In the *Winter's Tale* the thief Autolycus declares that "Though I am not naturally honest, I am so sometimes by chance" (4.4.715–16). He is the only person at the sheep-shearing festival who knows of Camillo's plot to help Florizel and Perdita run off together, but he refuses to inform on them to King Polixenes—"I hold it the more knavery to conceal it; and therein am I constant to my profession" (4.4.685–86). Not knowing what threat to "the Prince my master" the Shepherd and Clown's determination to acquaint the King with the fact of Perdita's being a foundling may pose, he decides to mislead the rustics (and to take their gold) and to put them on board the fleeing Florizel's ship rather than to take them to Polixenes, saying, "If I had a mind to be honest, I see Fortune would not suffer me; she drops booties in my mouth" (ll. 834–35). In his wonderment that his being "constant to my profession" of thievery leads him not only to wealth but to honest acts, Autolycus refers to both chance and fortune, appropriate for a man born under the sign of Mercury and so thoroughly immersed in the whirligig of time as he. But his rhetoric highlights the fact that his very practice of thievery is being used for good ends: the good is realized not in spite of his (admittedly humorous) evil ways but because of them.

The honest man, knowing no more of the facts of the situation at the festival than did Autolycus, would have stopped the Prince and Perdita from leaving. But it takes a thief to know better. For the "imperfection" of an Autolycus is one of the means by which the great reunions of the end of the play are achieved. "Chance" and "fortune" are changed in front of his (and the audience's) eyes into something more ordered and purposeful. Simon Palfrey says that Autolycus "parodies the genre's redemptive pretensions."[20] But surely redemption is no pretense in this genre as it is practiced by Shakespeare and what strikes Autolycus in this whole episode with the Shepherd and Clown is that he is caught up in a providential cycle without having to change his basic character.

In general, evil being turned into good is a favorite device of Shakespeare in the romances; his characters suffer many fortunate falls: the Roman commander Lucius tells the weeping Imogen, suffering over what she thought was the death of Posthumus, to "wipe thine eyes. / Some falls are means the happier to arise" (*Cymbeline*, 4.2.405–6), and in the late plays just about all falls are of this kind. This providential theme is of course found in earlier

Shakespeare as well, as when Duke Vicentio says to Marianna of the bed trick he contrives with her and Isabella against Angelo, "the justice of your title to him / Doth flourish the deceit" (*Measure for Measure*, 4.1.73–74). In *Cymbeline*, Imogen is lied to by beggars about where she can find some charitable foundations to supply her needs when she is wandering in Wales, but as a result of the deception she finds the cave of her lost brothers and Belarius, the beginning of the multiple reconciliations in this play. When she lies to Lucius about the name of the headless corpse that she finds beside her when she awakens from drinking Pisanio's potion, saying it was that of a "Richard du Champ," she consoles herself by saying, "If I do lie and do / No harm by it, though the gods hear, I hope / They'll pardon it" (4.2.380–82). (But of course had she told what she *thought* was the right name of the corpse, Posthumus, it would have been a "lie," too, or at least not factually correct; nothing she could have said in this situation, including, "I don't know who this corpse is"—she thought she did know—could have been true to the fact of its being Cloten. Even when Imogen thinks she is lying, in a sense she really is not.)

Villains, however, are not successful at this kind of providential direction of bringing good from evil. Cloten, for example, bungles his attempt. He says to Posthumus's loyal servant Pisanio that "what villainy soe'er I bid thee do, [so thou] perform it directly and truly—I would [then] think thee an honest man" (3.5.112–13). But Pisanio understands the relevant point: "for true to thee," he says in soliloquy at the end of the scene, "Were to prove false, which I will never be, / To him [Posthumus] that is most true" (ll. 158–59). Nonetheless Pisanio does lie to his master Posthumus when he says that Imogen was dead and also lies to his other master, the King, by saying that he does not know why Imogen left the court (he himself had arranged it). He in fact does not know what has become of either Imogen or Posthumus when he speaks to the King and sums up very well the situation of all those in the romances who are twisted and turned by fortune and the evil acts of others and who look to providence for resolution. Indeed, since fortune/destiny/fate is the instrument of providence it seems to be true in these plays that the more radically one experiences the turns of fortune's wheel, the better he will be able to see beyond to providence. For, as Pisanio says, he is "Perplexed in all. The heavens still must work. / Wherein I am false I am honest; not true, to be true," and he asks that all doubtful issues "by time let them be cleared; / Fortune brings in some boats that are not steered" (4.3.41–42, 45–46). Just about everyone in the romances, at one time or another, is like Pisanio here, or, to take an example from the joyous comedies, like Viola in *Twelfth Night*, sitting like Patience on her monument, smiling at grief.

And there are other examples of this important theme of evil turning into good in *Cymbeline*. It is addressed directly, for example, by Jupiter in the last act. The god is challenged by the ghostly "first brother" of Posthumus, who asks why all "the graces for his [Posthumus's] merits due" have been "all to dolors turned" (5.4.77–80). All of Jupiter's twenty-line response is relevant to our topic; among other things, he tells Posthumus' anxious (if deceased) family,

> Be not with mortal accidents oppressed
> No care of yours it is; you know 'tis ours.
> Whom best I love I cross, to make my gift,
> The more delayed, delighted.
>   (5.4.99–102)

Further, it is prophesied that Posthumus's own reunion with Imogen will be "happier much by his affliction made" (108). Similarly, in *Pericles* the hero is told by the goddess Diana that he must go to her temple at Ephesus "To mourn thy crosses, with thy daughter's, call / And give them repetition to the life" (5.1.248–49),[21] which, when he has done so and discovers his resurrected wife, he tells the gods that "Your present kindness / Makes my past miseries sports" (5.3.41–42).

Also, Posthumus' jailer, who watches over him after he has been captured by the British, has some Autolycus-like perplexities. Struck by his prisoner's resignation before he is scheduled to be hanged, he muses that "I would we were all of one mind, and one mind good. . . . . I speak against my present profit, but my wish hath a preferment in't" (5.4.203, 205–6)—that is, if all were good, he would be out of work, yet somehow this might be acceptable. Events are so complicated at the end of this play and also in *The Winter's Tale*—as of course they get in life as well—that both the jailer and Autolycus can see that in their pity for those apparently out of favor there is something that may also redound to their "preferment." Virtue may be its own reward, but in a providential universe it may be rewarded in more conventional ways as well—all the more remarkable in that those so rewarded may not be themselves conventionally "good" persons.

III. Providence and Shakespeare's Heroes

From the perspective of those who affirm providence, though, it is not necessary that all evil be turned to good, for they would say, simply, that it is better to suffer evil than to do it. Boethius is absolutely relentless in insisting that the bad man is more unhappy than the good, even when his schemes seem to come to success, and in this he is extending the thought of a classical precursor like Seneca, who claimed that "No evil can befall a good man; opposites do not mingle:"[22] any apparent evil that may come one's way is simply an opportunity to demonstrate virtue, which is the basis of nobility and true happiness. Boethius, through Lady Philosophy, says that it is "manifest that the good are never without rewards, nor the evil without punishments" (4.3; 315), in saying which he reaches beyond Seneca to Plato's *Gorgias*, which demonstrated that it was better to suffer evil than to do it. Kings, says Lady Philosophy,

> we behold
> In highest glory placed,
> And with rich purple graced,
> Compassed with soldiers bold;
> Whose countenance shows fierce threats,
> Who with rash fury chide,
> If any strip the pride
> From their vainglorious feats;
> He'll see them close oppressed
> Within by galling chains.
>   (4.3; 315)

This might describe many of Shakespeare's kings, certainly not least Leontes. He is also a vivid example of the Boethian view that "if it be a miserable thing to desire that which is evil, it is more miserable to be able to perform it" (4.4; 323), with the corollary that it is better for such a person then to suffer correction for the bad things that he has done, a function which of course Paulina willingly undertakes for Leontes. Again Boethius: "the wicked have some good annexed when they are punished, to wit, the punishment itself, which by reason of justice is good." (4.4; 327). Is Hermione also happier, better off, for her undeserved suffering than her husband Leontes, the inflicter of injustice and suffering, as the Boethian formula would suggest? The speeches of both would seem to affirm as much. Leontes' speech is notoriously crabbed and difficult to follow while Hermione says that the suffering she will undergo is for her "better grace" (*The Winter's Tale*, 2.1.123). At the time this was a statement of faith only, as she of course did not know how the present tragedies were to be redeemed; but in the conclusion of the play she will be not only a gracious royal personage, the Queen of Sicily and the daughter of the Emperor of Russia, but also the very embodiment of grace responsible for the happiness of all who know and love her.

Not only is it better to suffer evil than to do it; Boethius's spokeswoman Lady Philosophy also declares that "highest Providence often worketh that wonderful miracle, that evil men make those which are evil[,] good. For some, considering the injustice done them by most wicked men, inflamed with hatred of evildoers[,] have returned to the practice of virtue, procuring [i.e., seeking] to be contrary to them whom they hate" (4.6; 351). And here, I think, Boethius's high priestess has found a place even for *The Tempest*'s Caliban in her providential scheme. For is this not the context for his remarkable resolution in his last speech in the play, where he says that

> I'll be wise hereafter,
> And seek for grace. What a thrice-double ass
> Was I to take this drunkard for a god,
> And worship this dull fool [Stephano]!
> (5.1.295–98)

For St. Thomas Aquinas, providence involves two things: first, the orderly disposition of the universe, and second, the "execution of order, which is termed government. Of these, the first is eternal, and the second is temporal" (Pt. I, Q. 22, Art. 1). God, the universal cause, must necessarily direct all things towards the good—that is his nature, as Aquinas takes pains to show throughout the *Summa Theologica*, but he may also rely on secondary causes to be his temporal governors, such as human beings or impersonal forces such as fate or destiny. Fate, for example, he says, quoting the Boethian formulation, "is a disposition inherent to changeable things, by which Providence connects each one with its proper order" (Pt. I, Q. 116, Art. 1).

Several things are important here for Shakespeare's plays. Aquinas makes clear that God's goodness and glory are in fact increased, not diminished, by frequently having other agents execute his government, a significant distinction from the Puritans' emphasis on special providences and frequent direct supernatural interventions in day-to-day affairs. Taking the example of an earthly king, Aquinas says the fact that he "should have ministers to execute his laws" is a sign of his dignity, "because by the ordering of ministers the kingly power is brought into greater evidence" (Pt. I, Q. 103, Art. 6, Reply Obj. 3). This importance of creatures is clearly significant to things such as stage plays, and Shakespeare's skill in delineating human actions, from this perspective, would not detract from considerations of the divine government of the universe but could theoretically make such government more evident.

IV. Providence, Nature and Myth in the Late Plays

It is important to remember that when Shakespeare composed his late romances it was forbidden to "jestingly or prophanely speake or use the holy Name of God or of Christ Jesus, or of the Holy Ghoste or of the Trinitie, which are not to be spoken but with feare and reverence"—the famous "Act to Restrain Abuses of Players" passed by Parliament in 1606,[23] which had the effect of greatly reducing any references to the Christian deity. But because of the early seventeenth-century familiarity with the concept of providence it would be clear to an audience that when, for example, Prospero tells Miranda in *The Tempest* that they were brought to their almost deserted island "By Providence divine" (1.2.160), a well-known divine characteristic, or "minister," was being referred to without violating the legal taboo.

It is interesting to note, by the way, again in *Twelfth Night*, the contrast between a providence operating through various—and sometimes unlikely human agents—as opposed to the direct intervention favored by puritans. Malvolio, said by Maria to be a "kind of Puritan" (2.3.139), is one who thinks providence has tapped him rather decisively on the shoulder when he discovers what he thinks is his mistress Olivia's note confessing her love for him. Maurice Hunt has provided a good summary of the situation: In Malvolio, Shakespeare satirizes the "unmediated, unearned, material blessings of the elect." But the play as a whole "endorses a more removed, less easily knowable deity who works through secondary agents such as the sea to reward individuals who have had to earn their blessing by selflessly serving others."[24] Although I do not know that this deity is more removed or less knowable for working through secondary agents—could he not be just as easily seen as closer and more familiar?—Shakespeare does use in the romances all manner of natural events and persons to make providence known.

To think of *Twelfth Night* is also to be reminded that the workings of providence are strikingly manifested in travel, especially upon the sea. "If the sea is an emblem of dangerous chance," says Kathleen Williams, "it is also an emblem of the justice of Providence, working through apparent chance itself."[25] St. Paul's journey to Rome, recorded in the Acts of the Apostles (chapters 27–28), is one of the paradigms for this, as his intercessory prayer brings the ship he is traveling upon and all its passengers to safety at the island of Malta. Jonah's being thrown overboard and being preserved in the belly of the whale is another obvious example. In the Gospels, Christ rebukes the waves to calm the disciples during a particularly fierce storm and on another violent occasion walks on the water to their boat. Arion's being saved by the dolphins is a classical analog, referred to by the captain in *Twelfth Night* in describing for Viola the possible salvation of her brother during a storm at sea, as is Odysseus' receiving from the sea nymph Ino her girdle that allows him to land on the island of the Phaeacians, a refuge from the storm raised by Poseidon.

In Shakespeare's *Pericles* travel and providence are quite closely connected. Helicanus advises Pericles to escape the realm of Antiochus, the unjust and incestuous king, until his "rage and anger be forgot, / Or till the

Destinies do cut his thread of life" (1.2.109–10). That the "Destinies" are here the instruments of providence is apparent from Helicanus' subsequent theological description of the sad end of Antiochus, whose "greatness was no guard / To bar heaven's shaft, but sin had his reward" (2.4.14–15), recalling St. Paul's words in Romans, "The wages of sin is death" (6.23). Pericles' leaving of Tyre is also providential for Thaliard, who was dispatched from Antioch to kill him, and the would-be assassin's comment, "Well, I perceive / I shall not be hanged now, although I would" (1.3.25–26), that is, he was willing to put his head in the noose by killing Pericles but now realizes that forces outside his control have prevented this, is another example of the *topos* of one's doing right almost in spite of himself. And Pericles' journey is profitable not only for himself and Thaliard but also for Cleon and the famished people of Tarsus where he is sailing. His ships are not, says Pericles, a "Trojan horse" (1.4.93) designed to overthrow Cleon's government but are rather "stored with corn to make your needy bread / And give them life whom hunger starved half dead" (1.4.95–96). Pericles says that he and his men will "feast here awhile, / Until our stars that frown lend us a smile" (1.4.108–9).

This last statement is similar to Hermione's saying, upon being accused of adultery by Leontes, "I must be patient till the heavens look / With an aspect more favorable" (2.1.106–7), and to Prospero's conviction that he must act swiftly to achieve his ends because he knows "by my prescience" (1.2.181)—recalling that this was what Raleigh in 1614 called God's foreseeing the future—that his fortune depends upon "A most auspicious star" (l. 183) which if he does not follow will cause that fortune to "ever after droop" (l. 185). All these are examples of how thoroughly Shakespeare calls attention to Boethius' doctrine that destiny, fortune, and the stars are the instruments of providence. That providence does lie behind these things and uses them for its own purposes is clear from the happy ending of all the romances; fate and the stars are not accustomed on their own to achieving benign purposes. Chaucer, too, in one of his most providential stories, the "Man of Law's Tale," had closely juxtaposed the stars and providence. The Man of Law says that perhaps it was written in the stars that the Syrian Sultan, who desired to marry the story's heroine, Constance, should die for love, for "in the sterres, clerer than is glas, / Is writen, God woot, whoso koude it rede, / The deeth of every man" (ll. 194–96),[26] but to understand the reason Constance herself was not killed by the Sultan's enraged mother-in-law (who objected to the marriage, to say the least, on religious grounds) it is necessary to look beyond the stars. It was because Christ:

Dooth thyng for certein ende that ful derk is
To mannes wit, that for oure ignorance

Ne konne noght knowe his prudent purveiance [providence].
   (ll. 481–83)

In Shakespeare, indeed, it is *The Tempest* that most clearly reveals the complex but coherent interdependence of the forces which we are describing.
Prospero affirms the providential nature of his magic to Miranda in the first
act. He says that he has with

> Such provision in mine art
> So safely ordered that there is no soul—
> No, not so much perdition as an hair
> Betid to any creature in the vessel
> Which thou heardst cry.
>   (1.2.28–32)

Here is very likely a reference to significant texts about providence in the
New Testament: Luke 21.18, in which Christ says to his disciples about
future persecutions, "there shall not one hair of your heads perish," as well
as to Acts 27.34, St. Paul's similar words of consolation to those sailing with
him on tempestuous seas. Reinforcing the theme is Ariel's later saying to
Prospero that "not a hair perished" (l. 218) of those on the ship.

The providential nature of the enforced travel of Prospero and Miranda
themselves is also clear from their dialog. Miranda asks whether they left
Milan by foul play, "Or blessed was 't we did" (ll. 60–61), and her father
answers that it was both: "By foul play, as thou sayst, were we heaved thence, /
But blessedly holp hither" (ll. 62–63), and here again is the familiar theme of
good coming from evil: evil turns of the wheel of fortune serve only to reveal
the Boethian providence that keeps it balanced.

Gonzalo says that he and his "friends'" preservation from the sea was
a "miracle" (2.1.6), and he frequently speaks, as noted earlier, in providential
terms. In reviewing in Act 5 the events that have taken place, he says that
"Claribel her husband" found at Tunis and Ferdinand, her brother, a wife,
"Where he himself was lost; Prospero his dukedom / In a poor isle; and all
of us ourselves / When no man was his own" (5.1.210–15). This seems to
refer to Matthew 16.25, where Christ talks of those who must lose their lives
in order to save them, a paradox that surely depends on providential aid for
its fulfillment. Gonzalo also notices that their garments are fresh after the
tempest—"being rather new-dyed than stained with salt water" (2.1.66–67).
He of course also imagines the kind of government he would establish on
the island, claiming that he "would with such perfection govern . . . T'excel
the Golden Age" (2.1.169–70). But providence is not in the business of

establishing utopias but rather in reinvigorating or newly establishing those who would govern existing states.

Shakespeare is particularly skillful in Act 3 in tying together the themes we are examining when Ariel, dressed as a harpy, causes the magical banquet that had attracted Alonso to disappear and the spirit then speaks authoritatively to the King of Naples, Prospero's brother Antonio, and Alonso's brother Sebastian: they are, he says,

> three men of sin, whom Destiny—
> That hath to instrument this lower world
> And what is in't—the never surfeited sea
> Hath caused to belch up you.
> (3.3.53–56)

The Boethian context is clear here—destiny acting as the instrument of providence, itself using "this lower world," in particular the sea, as its own instrument. Ariel's calling the villains "men of sin" is a strong phrase and is a connection of destiny and sin similar to that in *Pericles*. But as is Shakespeare's custom, he thoroughly portrays the natural (or classical) context of an action before venturing towards the supernatural (or Christian). As befits his classical disguise as a harpy, then, and therefore a spokesman for fate, Ariel tells his victims that "I have made you mad; / And even with suchlike valor men hang and drown / Their proper selves" (3.3.58–60). To reinforce the classical context, he next tells them, after they draw their swords against him, that "I and my fellows / Are ministers of Fate" (ll. 60–61); destiny and fate, then, are powers portrayed as the villains' nemesis, inexorable and destructive, which have delayed but not forgotten their crimes and have "Incensed the seas and shores, yea, all the creatures / Against your peace" (ll. 73–75), which do pronounce

> by me
> Lingering perdition, worse than any death
> Can be at once, [and] shall step by step attend
> You and your ways.
> (ll. 76–79)

Retribution for the death of Agamemnon or for Oedipus's killing of Laius and marriage to Jocasta could hardly have been announced more grimly. But then Ariel speaks in another vein at the end of his condemnation, which is crucial: the powers' vengeance can be avoided by "heart's sorrow / And a clear life ensuing" (ll. 81–82), a penitential note that suggests the Boethian framework in which destiny and fate are classical ministers that serve as transparencies to a higher, more merciful intelligence.

There are also figures of anti-providence in the romances, who can help us to understand the positive types. The Queen in *Cymbeline* is preeminent among these. Imogen's first words in the play describe her stepmother's hypocrisy as she exclaims against "Dissembling courtesy! How fine this tyrant / Can tickle where she wounds" (1.1.85–86). The Queen is opposite to Autolycus: as he cannot do harm without having it converted to good, she says that she never does the King wrong "But he does buy my injuries, to be friends" (1.1.106). It is not providence here that converts evil into good, as is the case for an Autolycus, but rather a shallow King, who cannot see through the pretenses of his wife. The Queen is a parody of providence. She appears good but acts the reverse; indeed, she delights in pointing publicly to the possible malicious irony of her actions, telling the doctor Cornelius that he should give her poisons for experiments, "unless thou think'st me devilish" (1.5.16)—which she pretends is a kind of absurdity but which Cornelius wisely takes seriously. He does not give her a fatal poison but one that only locks up the patient's senses for a while, commenting that "She is fooled / With a most false effect, and I the truer / So to be false with her" (ll. 43–44), a familiar dynamic in the drama of providence. It is this action that of course preserves later the life of Imogen.

The doctor's actions illustrate that in romance good no less than evil may mock appearances and may seem what it is not in order to bring about justice, just as Hamlet learns he must in fact "seem" to be other than he is in order to survive at Elsinore, and this is another characteristic of providence in the romances. In general, Christ's injunction to the disciples to be "Wise as serpents" (Matthew 10.16) is followed by the virtuous in the romances, certainly to a greater degree than we see in tragic heroes such as Othello or in Gloucester and Lear. But the romantic characters illustrate as well the other half of the divine injunction, to be as "innocent as doves," as they do not pursue malice. This mildness of virtue is partly why its true qualities remain hidden. God as the "deus absconditus," the hidden God, is a consistent theme in the Bible ("Is not this the carpenter's son?" [Matthew 13.55]), and Shakespeare, too, loves the device of hidden virtue: evil is not to have all the fun of pretending to be what it is not.[27]

From a biblical perspective to do good in secret seems to be essential to receiving a providential reward. Christ tells his hearers in the Sermon on the Mount to pray, not in a long-winded and public manner as do the Pharisees but rather to go into a private room and shut the door and that their father, who hears in secret, will reward them. The person who would do good must not let his right hand know what his left hand is doing. Good works then will proceed naturally, without fanfare, like the Kingdom of Heaven, which manifests itself obscurely like the yeast in a lump of dough or the tiny mustard seed that becomes a grand tree. Virtue which is so hidden that it is almost extinguished is, of course, commonplace in the romances. Cymbeline's sons are raised in obscurity in Wales and appear in public just in time to save (along with their old foster father Belarius and the disguised Posthumous Leonatus) the British army. Perdita is raised in obscurity—albeit a wealthy one—in Bohemia and Imogen, although raised at court, goes into disguise as a boy when her husband seeks her life. Marina's virtue in *Pericles* is most astonishing of all, displayed as it is in a brothel, where her eloquence amazingly saves her from violation. And while living in obscurity makes such persons' advancement in the world less likely, it also paradoxically makes their virtue more striking: Perdita's candid recognition that she is the equal of Polixenes ("The selfsame sun that shines upon his court / Hides not his visage from our cottage" [*The Winter's Tale*, 4.4.446–47]), Marina's speeches to her customers, especially to the governor of Mytilene, Lysimachus, which causes him to fall in love with her ("Had I brought hither a corrupted mind, / Thy speech had altered it" [*Pericles*, 4.6.105–6]), Miranda's recognition in *The Tempest* that Ferdinand was only the "third man that e'er I saw, the first / That e'er I sighed for" (1.2.449–50) and her consequent charmingly bold courtship of him, undeterred by social convention. Their actions here are certainly a reflection of their own character but their clarity and forthrightness is perhaps also a reflection of a virtue that has been nourished and cultivated in private circumstances: as Adam says in *Paradise Lost*, "sometimes solitude is sweet society" (9.249).

Also, the sheer number of times that the gods and the heavens are invoked indicates the pervasiveness of providence in the romances. To look, briefly, only at *Cymbeline*: first, the unnamed "Second Gentleman" breaks into verse to offer this prayer for Imogen: "The heavens hold firm / The walls of thy dear honor" (2.1.62–63). Then, Imogen in the next scene seconds this notion when she lays aside the book that she had been reading and says, "To your protection I commend me, gods" (2.2.8). She needs (and receives) their protection, as Iachimo then leaves the trunk in which he had gained access to her bedroom to spy on her while she is sleeping—but does not rape her. Imogen also invokes the "good gods" (3.2.29; cf. 3.2.39) that the news contained in Posthumus' letter to her may be beneficial, and Posthumus says that in the fight against the Romans, "all was lost, / But that the heavens fought" (5.3.3–4). In the astonishing last act Cymbeline says there was no way he could have detected his Queen's perfidy and prays, "Heaven mend all" (5.5.69). To all those that are reunited he proposes that they "smoke the temple with our sacrifices" (5.5.402). When he says that he will submit to Rome even though he has won the war, the Soothsayer concludes that "The fingers of the powers above do tune / The harmony of this peace" (ll. 470–71).

A final important feature of providence that illuminates aspects of the romances is its connection to art and prudence. Harriet Hawkins has said that "the major word associated with [Prospero] is not 'providence' but 'Art.'"[28] In fact the two act in complementary ways both in the play and in the philosophical tradition behind it. St. Thomas Aquinas, for one, has pointed out some of these affinities. For St. Thomas, says one of his modern interpreters, the divine knowledge and the divine will are key elements in the construction of his notion of providence: "divine knowledge is the cause of all things when the divine will is joined to it, just as the knowledge of the artist is the cause of his work of art when there is added to it an inclination to that effect, which inclination is through his will."[29] This is still the case for Shakespeare's age; in Golding's *De Mornay* (ix, 1587), for example, cited in the *Oxford English Dictionary*, is the statement, "What else is Providence, than the will of God uttered foorth with Reason, and orderly disposed by understanding?"[30]

St. Thomas also links closely the moral virtue of prudence to his doctrine of providence, saying that prudence is "the remembrance of the past, and understanding of the present" from which "we gather how to provide for the future" (Pt. I, Q. 22, Art. 1). In *The Tempest*, then, Prospero's art, his magic, does indeed contrive to put all his enemies at his mercy but what is to be done with them is a question that his art cannot answer; it is rather a matter of morality whether or not to seek vengeance for the wrong done to him. In God's providence both are inherently united: everything that exists is oriented or artistically disposed toward the good and it is to achieve this coherence that an earthly figure such as Prospero ultimately decides that the "rarer action is / In virtue than in vengeance." He "savor[s] as much of Judeo-Christian divinity as dramatic credibility will allow," says John B. Bender, and never is this more true than his decision here.[31]

Or, again, art and morality work together to achieve a providential end in *The Winter's Tale*. The statue of Hermione, a work of art, is regarded by all who look on it as exceedingly well done, particularly in its life-likeness, but these noble persons are far from mere aesthetic spectators; to see the statue is for Leontes to be reminded of his past sins, never far, of course, from his mind, of the wrong choices of his moral life. That the statue "comes alive" and makes possible the providential reconciliations of the play's end is a sign that Leontes' penance has been sufficient and that art and morality are united in a new way: things made (art) and things done (penance) are one. Prudence for the Renaissance had the strong sense of realizing the good, not our own time's weak sense of "taking no risks," and Shakespeare's artistic plots with their giving often undeserving subjects second and third chances still require of those persons conscious moral choices. We have already looked at a number of examples: Caliban's remarkable confession that he will sue for grace at the end of *The Tempest*; Alonso's guilty conscience that makes him quick to repent; Leontes' steadfastness in penance for sixteen years under the lash of Paulina's tongue; and in addition to these there is Iachimo's repenting his lies about Imogen ("Pardon is the word to all," says Cymbeline, [5.5.425]) and Posthumus' forbearing to take Iachimo's life on the battlefield when circumstances were certainly conducive to so doing—he was in disguise, they were fighting in opposed armies.

This union of art and morality[32]—of "mouldy tales," as Ben Jonson famously called *Pericles*, and the comedy of forgiveness, to use Robert Hunter's fine phrase—is what gives the providential sense to these plays. For surely even Jonson would have agreed that the history of the world itself is a pretty mouldy tale, yet it is that which divine providence undertakes to direct to a supernatural end and to do so through the free choices of men and women who, fortunately, on occasion practice forgiveness and forbearance, who see beyond fate and destiny—while never circumventing them—to providence.[33] "Only to Man thou hast made known thy ways," says George Herbert, "And put the pen alone into his hand / And made him Secretary of thy praise" ("Providence," 6–8). Shakespeare was not the least of those who have held that office.

NOTES

1. *Marlowe's Tamberlaine: A Study in Renaissance Moral Philosophy* (Nashville, Tenn.: Vanderbilt University Press, 1964), 86.

2. Antonio Poppi, "Fate, Fortune, Providence and Human Freedom," *The Cambridge History of Renaissance Philosophy*, ed. Charles B. Schmitt, et al. (Cambridge, U.K.: Cambridge University Press, 1988), 667.

3. Beverly Kennedy, *Knighthood in the Morte D'Arthur* (Cambridge, U.K.: D. S. Brewer, 1985), 336. Kennedy calls this a "providentialist" view.

4. "Providence, Authority, and the Moral Life in *The Tempest*," *Shakespeare Studies* 16 (1983): 237, 249.

5. "Providence by Indirection in Seventeenth-Century Tragicomedy," in *Drama and Religion*, James Redmond, ed. (Cambridge, U.K.: Cambridge University Press, 1983), 39. In earlier sixteenth-century humanistic biblical plays, divine providence played an important role; for example, Ruth Blackburn says that the "Joseph plays by Crocus, Fischlin, Macropedius, and others bring out this point very clearly. . . . . God's providence guides men" (*Biblical Drama under the Tudors* [The Hague: Mouton, 1971], 78).

6. Margaret J. Osler, *Divine Will and the Mechanical Philosophy: Gassendi and Descartes on Contingency and Necessity in the Created World* (Cambridge, U.K.: Cambridge University Press, 1994), 56.

7. *Cambridge History of Renaissance Philosophy*, 642.

8. *The Consolation of Philosophy*, trans. I.T., 1609, in Loeb Classical Library (Cambridge, Mass.: Harvard University Press, 1918), translation revised by H. F. Stewart, 341 [Bk. 4, ch. 6]. Subsequent quotations are to this edition and are included in the text; citations indicate book and section numbers, followed by page numbers. According to Chauncey Wood, "Boethius wished to deny that there is such a thing as 'fate' by showing that what we call fate is really the temporal operation of providence" (*Chaucer and the Country of the Stars* [Princeton, N.J.: Princeton University Press, 1970], 33).

9. See Bertram Joseph, *Conscience and the King* (London: Chatto and Windus, 1953), 133.

10. *Of the Laws of Ecclesiastical Polity* (New York: E. P. Dutton, 1964), I, 159–60. Subsequent references are in the text and refer to the page numbers of this edition.

11. Introduction, *The Countess of Pembroke's Arcadia* (London: Penguin, 1977), 35.

12. *The Works of Sir Walter Ralegh* (Oxford, U.K.: The University Press, 1829), II, 34.

13. *Harvard Classics*, ed. Charles W. Eliot (New York: P. F. Collier, 1909), III, 42.

14. *The Sermons of John Donne*, eds. George R. Potter and Evelyn M. Simpson (Berkeley: University of California Press, 1962), III, 358. Calvin also agrees with Donne on this point: "Moreover, to make God a momentary Creator, who once for all finished, would be cold and barren, and we must differ from profane men especially in that we see the presence of divine power shining as much in the continuing state of the universe as in its inception" (*Institutes*, I, xvi.1; quoted in Horton Davies, *The Vigilant God: Providence in the Thought of Augustine, Aquinas, Calvin and Barth* [New York: Peter Lang, 1992], 96.)

15. All quotations from Shakespeare are from *The Complete Works of Shakespeare*, David Bevington, ed. (New York: Addison Wesley Longman, 1997).

16. *George Herbert*, ed. Louis Martz (Oxford, U.K.: Oxford University Press, 1994), 100.

17. Anthony Low, "Sin, Penance, and Privatization in the Renaissance," *Ben Jonson Journal* 5 (1998): 11. Low cites a number of sources to support this statement.

18. *The Works of Sir Walter Ralegh*, II, 39.

19. *Summa Theologica*, trans. Fathers of the English Dominican Province (Westminster, Md.: Christian Classics, 1981; orig. pub. 1911), I, 566 (Pt. I, Q. 116, Art. 1). All subsequent quotations from St. Thomas are from this work and are included in the text. John P. Rock suggests that for St. Thomas, "The very name of God means Providence" ("Divine Providence in St. Thomas Aquinas," *Boston College Studies in Philosophy* [1966]: 70; he cites Pt. I, Q. 13, Art. 8 of the *Summa*).

20. *Late Shakespeare: A New World of Words* (Oxford, U.K.: Clarendon Press, 1997), 238.

21. "The hero of late Shakespearean romance learns that metaphysical evil is not evil after all. Rather, it consists of 'crosses' that a ruling god or goddesses lays upon him in order to make his final joys more delightful for having been delayed" (Maurice Hunt, *Shakespeare's Romance of the Word* [Lewisburg: Bucknell University Press, 1990], 31). In the printed 1599 text of the dramatic romance *Sir Clyomon and Sir Clamydes* the heroine, thinking that her lover is dead, is about to commit suicide

when Providence itself descends from the heavens and assures her that he is still alive.

22. *On Providence*, trans. John W. Basore (Cambridge, Mass.: Harvard University Press, 1913), 2.1.

23. The "Act" is quoted in Richard Dutton, *Mastering the Revels* (Iowa City, Iowa: University of Iowa Press, 1991), 162. Dutton also says there: "The dramatists' increased use after 1606 of classical or pagan settings for their plays may be a token of the profession's own efforts not to offend in these matters."

24. "Malvolio, Viola, and the Question of Instrumentality: Defining Providence in Twelfth Night," *Studies in Philology* 90 (1993): 278.

25. "Spenser: Some Uses of the Sea and the Storm-tossed Ship," *Research Opportunities in Renaissance Drama* 13–14 (1970–71): 137. Great storms at sea were "the usual Shakespearean image for the power of nature over human life" (Alvin Kernan, *The Playwright as Magician* [New Haven, Conn.: Yale University Press, 1979], 139).

26. *The Works of Geoffrey Chaucer*, ed. F. N. Robinson (Cambridge, Mass.: The Riverside Press, 1957). Subsequent references are to this edition.

27. Some of G. K. Chesterton's fictional works are very much in this spirit. The policemen in *The Man Who Was Thursday*, for example, are allowed to know something of the wild anarchy of being a terrorist and the husband and wife in *Manalive* run off with one another again and again in different disguises in town after town.

28. "Fabulous Counterfeits: Dramatic Construction and Dramatic Perspectives in *The Spanish Tragedy, A Midsummer Night's Dream*, and *The Tempest*," *Shakespeare Studies* 6 (1970): 58.

29. Walter L. Ysaac, "The Certitude of Providence in St. Thomas," *The Modern Schoolman* (1961): 318.

30. This illustrative quotation is under definition 3, which defines divine providence as "The foreknowing and beneficent care and government of God (or of nature, etc.); divine direction, control, or guidance."

31. "The Day of *The Tempest*," *ELH* 47 (1980): 242–43.

32. Howard Felperin suggests that "Shakespeare reassigns the role once played by the grace of God to the art of man: the role of raising and reforming mere nature" ("Undream'd Shores: *The Tempest*," in *Dramatic Romance: Plays, Theory, and Criticism* [New York: Harcourt Brace Jovanovich, 1973], 222). This is a view that continues to attract critics; Cynthia Marshall, for example, says that "The theater came to approximate, in an age when doubt and faith were drawing into closer balance, many of the functions traditionally met by the Church" (*Last Things and Last Plays: Shakespearean Eschatology* [Carbondale and Edwardsville, Ill.: Southern Illinois Press, 1991], 111). But surely these claims are dubious. There is nothing in the plays that suggests that art by itself has a true supernatural function—that it can change or transform human nature, which is the nature of charity and grace—quite the contrary, really. Prospero's epilogue, for example, makes clear that he needs all the help he can get in his reintroduction to normal life. And the whole point about the artist Julio Romano's "statue" in *The Winter's Tale* is that it is no statue. Drama may narrate, reenact, portray things rich and strange—but to "create" them? Where is there any evidence that Shakespeare thinks he is substituting art for theology?

33. In writing about *Richard III, Julius Caesar*, and *Macbeth*, Donald V. Stump says that "Free human will carrying out the cause of divine providence seems to have

fascinated Shakespeare" ("Hamlet, Cain and Abel and the Pattern of Divine Providence," *Renaissance Papers* [1985]: 33). Of course there has also been much written about the role of providence in the history plays. Henry Ansgar Kelly provides a wise summation of the evidence: "the sentiments of the Lancaster myth are spoken by Lancastrians, and opposing views are voiced by anti-Lancastrians and Yorkists. And the Tudor myth finds its fullest statement in the mouth of Henry Tudor." Shakespeare "leaves the question open as to how God would distribute praise and blame and sanctions for good and evil," although Kelly acknowledges that there are "exceptional cases" like *Henry V* and *Richard III* where everyone has the same idea about a character (*Divine Providence in the England of Shakespeare's Histories* [Cambridge, Mass.: Harvard University Press, 1970], 305–6). A more recent assessment of the evidence suggests "That Shakespeare assumed an underlying hidden providence at work in history may . . . be taken as a given, yet without submitting to a doctrine of passive obedience to the state" (James Alfred Lewin, *Ghosts of the Body-Politic: Shakespeare, Providence and Legitimacy*, Dissertation, University of Illinois at Chicago [1994], 4).

ALEXANDER LEGGATT

In the Shadow of Hamlet: Comedy and Death in All's Well That Ends Well

The opening of *All's Well That Ends Well*, with Bertram, the Countess, Helen, and Lafeu "*all in black*" (1.1.0 stage direction),[1] might suggest the opening of a tragedy, with the stage hung in black; or the funereal opening of *1 Henry VI*: "Hung be the heavens with black" (1.1.1). Costumes create the same brooding effect as stage decor. To J. L. Styan, the "suppressed. . . . feelings" and "uneasy relationships" of the scene itself suggest Ibsen.[2] The Shakespearean tragedy most closely echoed is of course *Hamlet*:

> COUNTESS . . . No more of this, Helen. Go to, no more, lest it
> be rather thought you affect a sorrow than to have—
> HELEN I do affect a sorrow indeed, but I have it too.
> LAFEU Moderate lamentation is the right of the dead, excessive
> grief the enemy of the living.
> (1.1.51–56)

The Countess and Lafeu seem to be striking the same note as Claudius and Gertrude: life has to go on. Helen claims, with Hamlet, that beneath the surface of mourning is real grief, "That within which passes show" (1.2.85). Continuing the *Hamlet* link, the Countess gives Bertram parting advice that echoes the caution and prudence of Polonius addressing Laertes (1.1.64–70).

From *Re-Visions of Shakespeare: Essays in Honor of Robert Ornstein*, edited by Evelyn Gajowksi, pp. 231–42. Copyright © 2004 by Rosemont Publishing and Printing.

139

Yet while the shadow of *Hamlet* lies on this scene, the title advertises a comedy. The sorrow Helen affects, we learn shortly, is for the death of her father; the sorrow she really has is for Bertram's departure. Comedy may begin with memories of lost fathers, mothers, brothers, or sisters: as far back as *The Comedy of Errors* and as recently as *As You Like It* and *Twelfth Night*, Shakespeare was beginning comedies with young people touched by such losses. But Rosalind's interest turns to Orlando, Viola's to Orsino, Olivia's to Cesario. A characteristic pivotal line is Rosalind's "what talk we of fathers, when there is such a man as Orlando?" (3.4.36–37). When Helen declares in soliloquy, "I think not of my father" (1.1.81) and goes on to express her longing for Bertram, *All's Well* seems to be moving in the same direction. The way she cuts the Countess off in midsentence suggests the impatience of the young faced with the good advice of the elderly. And yet the Countess was advising her to moderate her grief, and her impatience has the same ground as Hamlet's impatience with Claudius and Gertrude. The turn to comic action is accompanied by a feeling akin to that of tragedy.

There is something strange about that opening stage direction: "*all in black.*" Taken literally, this means that even Lafeu, who has come to fetch Bertram to begin a new life at court, and who has suffered no bereavement we know of, is in mourning. The effect is radically different from act 1, scene 2 of *Hamlet*, where the Prince's mourning black stands out against the finery of the court. Here the whole onstage community, the whole world of the play as we see it in the opening scene, is touched by death. The Countess opens the play with a line that conflates birth and death in a complex paradox: "In delivering my son from me, I bury a second husband" (1.1.1–2).[3] Even for Bertram, the new life that is beginning is a replay of his loss: "And I, in going, madam, weep o'er my father's death anew" (1.1.3–4). The start of a new life is bound up with the end of an old one, as at the end of *Love's Labor's Lost*, where we learn in rapid succession that Jacquenetta is quick and the King of France is dead. Helen's grief over Bertram, which should be the start of a love-plot leading to new life, is conflated with her grief for the father she claims to have forgotten: "these great tears grace his remembrance more / Than those I shed for him" (1.1.82–83). Helen claims to have one real grief and one that is only apparent; but in this cryptic line, with its ambiguous pronouns, it is hard to tell them apart.[4] The impulses that might lead to new life are inextricably tangled with the thought of death.

In the atmosphere thus created, references to death that might otherwise be conventional hyperbole come closer to having a literal force. Bertram's departure is death for Helen: "There is no living, none, / If Bertram be away" (1.1.86–87). The hopelessness of her love is likewise death: "The hind that would be mated by the lion / Must die for love" (1.1.93–94). Her worship is devotion to a saint, a commemoration of the dead: "But now he's gone, and my idolatrous fancy / Must sanctify his relics" (1.1.99–100). Even later, when she has won the right to claim him as a husband, the chill of death touches her fear of rejection:

> The blushes in my cheeks thus whisper me:
> "We blush that thou shouldst choose; but, be refused,
> Let the white death sit on thy cheek for ever,
> We'll ne'er come there again."
>   (2.3.70–73)

In the subsequent action this link between Bertram's rejection and Helen's death will no longer be a figure of speech; it will be part of the story. For Paroles virginity is a kind of death: "He that hangs himself is a virgin: virginity murders itself" (1.1.140–41). Bertram will use a similar argument on Diana:

> If the quick fire of youth light not your mind
> You are no maiden but a monument.
> When you are dead you should be such a one
> As you are now; for you are cold and stern.
>   (4.2.5–8)

To be disappointed or unfulfilled in love is a sort of death. The idea is conventional enough. What makes *All's Well That Ends Well* special in this regard is that all these threatened, figurative deaths are anchored by memories of real deaths, and by the real experience of mourning.

In the opening scene Lafeu claims the King will be a new husband for the Countess, a new father for Bertram (1.1.7–8). He tries to make Bertram's condition as a ward sound like the creation of a new family to repair the loss. But as Bertram sees it, he will be "evermore in subjection" (1.1.5–6), as though he sees no end to the restrictions on his life imposed by the King's authority. The King himself, we learn in the same scene, is equally trapped by an incurable illness that gives him no choice but to wait for death. The court, which might have appeared to offer new life for Bertram, offers only stasis. In fact when the King first appears he seems brisk and businesslike, giving the latest war news, defining France's position, and declaring the freedom of his gentry to fight on either side. For the first fifteen lines of act 1, scene 2 we would not think we were listening to an ailing monarch. Then Bertram enters. The King immediately becomes melancholy and nostalgic, mourning the lost Count, complaining there is no one now who lives up to his standard, dwelling on his own illness and finally wishing for death (1.2.64–67). It is as though the sight of Bertram, who bears his father's face (1.2.19), turns the King into an old man. In the scene that follows Helen has a similar effect on the Countess; the young woman's love-grief stirs memories: "Even so it was with me when I was young" (1.3.128). The young, stirring memories in the old, make them feel their age.

Bertram brings his father's face to court, and starts a wave of nostalgia. Helen comes to court to cure the King and win a husband; in short, to get life moving again. But she brings with her one of her father's cures, which he gave to her on his deathbed (2.1.102). In the first scene she asked, "What was he like? / I have forgot him" (1.1.83–84); but she remembers his work well enough.[5] The King remembers her father as admiringly as he remembers Bertram's. He says of the Count, "It much repairs me / To talk of your good father" (1.2.30–31), and of Gérard de Narbon, "If he were living, I would try him yet" (1.2.72), as though he too could repair him. Through Helen's application of the cure, he does; it is as though the past has come to life to redeem the present, the dead to save the living.

Helen's plan, however, meets with some initial skepticism from the Countess and considerable resistance from the King. She wins them both over by the same means, by putting her own life on the line. The clinching argument for the Countess is:

> I'd venture
> The well-lost life of mine on his grace's cure
> By such a day, an hour.
>   (1.3.247–49)

Her way of going into new life involves confronting death, this time her own death, as well as using a cure given to her by a dying man. The King is more stubborn than the Countess, and makes her work harder. The same offer wins him, but she adds a new dimension to it:

> KING Upon thy certainty and confidence
> What dar'st thou venture?
> HELEN Tax of impudence,
> A strumpet's boldness, a divulgèd shame;
> Traduced by odious ballads, my maiden's name
> Seared otherwise; no worse of worst, extended
> With vilest torture, let my life be ended.
>   (2.1.167–72)

She puts death in the climactic position, and this is the offer that impresses the King: "Thy life is dear, for all that life can rate / Worth name of life in thee hath estimate" (2.1.177–78). He says nothing of her offer of sexual disgrace; she has actually dwelt on that longer than she dwells on death, however, and what he admires in her includes her youth and beauty (2.1:179).

What is going on here? Lafeu leaves the King and Helen together with a bawdy joke: "I am Cressid's uncle / That dare leave two together" (2.1.95–96). It is not that the King is a lecherous old man and the ensuing scene is a seduction, but it matters (as it matters when Isabella goes to plead with Angelo) that Helen is an attractive young woman. This, as well as her language, catches the King's attention, and her offer to squander that youth and beauty in death puts those qualities in high relief. Her offer to endure a strumpet's shame, and her implicit equation of this with death, anticipate the bed-trick when Helen, apparently (but not really) dead, will commit with Bertram an act that is apparently (but not really) fornication, and will undergo the figurative death of orgasm. The episodes are linked: Helen must win one man, the King, on the way to winning another, Bertram. When Bertram objects to the linking his language has sexual overtones: "But follows it, my lord, to bring me down / Must answer for your raising?" (2.3.113–14). She has restored the king's vigor, but she will deplete Bertram's when he undergoes his own orgasmic death with her. Bertram unconsciously acknowledges this link when he pleads with Diana, "give thyself unto my sick desires, / Who then recovers" (4.2.35–36). He wants Diana to cure him, as Helen cured the King, but once again it is Helen who will effect the cure.

Helen wins the King through a literal confrontation with death that has sexual overtones; as the King puts it, "Sweet practiser, thy physic I will try / That ministers thine own death if I die" (2.1.183–84). She will win Bertram through a literal act of sex that is figuratively an experience of death. She herself is careful to keep her relations with the King and her relations with Bertram separate. The King's speech might suggest that they will "die" together in sexual fulfilment; she reminds him that death in this case is not the sign of success but the punishment for failure: "Not helping, death's my fee." In the next line, completing the rhyme, she goes to the next item on her agenda: "But, if I help, what do you promise me?" (2.1.187–88). To cure the King she is willing to confront death, but her reason for curing the King, as she has frankly admitted to the Countess, is to win Bertram (1.3.231–35). It is the old romantic theme, the knight risking death to win the lady, but it is the old romantic theme with the sexes reversed, and Bertram, who has not set the conditions of the task himself, refuses to abide by them.

Instead he sets conditions that seem impossible, and the gulf that opens between them looks wider than ever. Yet in the painful aftermath of the wedding Helen and Bertram, literally far apart, are figuratively joined. Carrying on from the risk that Helen took in curing the King, they are linked through the way they confront death together. The link is anticipated by echoing language. Bertram's flight to the war is a plan he had in mind even before Helen came to Court: "By heaven, I'll steal away!" (2.1.33); Helen announces her own departure into apparent death with similar words: "with the dark, poor thief, I'll steal away" (3.2.129). As at the opening of the play Bertram's loss seemed to Helen like her own death, now it seems like his: "Madam, my lord is gone, for ever gone" (3.2.46). Forever gone: so we speak of the dead. Literally, he is risking his life in war, and Helen feels responsible: "Whoever shoots at him, I set him there" (3.2.112). In the letter she sends to the Countess she equates herself with death, and embraces her own death to prevent his: "He is too good and fair for death, and me, / Whom I myself embrace to set him free" (3.4.16–17). He goes to war, where he risks death as she did; meanwhile she reports her own death.

To the familiar equation of sex and death *All's Well* adds the equation of sex and war. This too is familiar, and Shakespeare has used it before: as Henry V moves toward the conquest of France, the Princess of France learns English words for the parts of her own body. Here the equation is both figurative and literal: Bertram's attempted conquest of Diana is metaphorically a siege; it is also part of the disillusioned realism of the war sequence, a recognizable tale of soldiers in their off hours.[6] Paroles and the Clown link sex and war with characteristic jokes. Paroles advises Helen that "Man setting down before you will undermine you and blow you up" (1.1.120–21). As he stresses the danger to women in sex that is figuratively war, the Clown stresses the danger to men in war that is figuratively sex: "The danger is in standing to't; that's the loss of men, though it be the getting of children" (3.2.41–42). Bertram and Helen, in effect, are endangered together.

The first report of Helen's death comes between Bertram's seduction of Diana and the gulling of Paroles, and coincides with the time when Bertram and Helen are in bed together. Bertram reports a busy night:

> I have congeed with the Duke, done my adieu with his nearest, buried a wife, mourned for her, writ to my lady mother I am returning, entertained my convoy, and between these main parcels of dispatch effected many nicer needs. The last was the greatest, but that I have not ended yet . . . as fearing to hear of it hereafter.
>
> (4.3.87–97)

He does. His fear is that Diana is pregnant; callow seducer though he is, he must have noticed that the woman he was having sex with had an orgasm, and medical belief in Shakespeare's time held that without an orgasm a woman could not conceive.[7] At the end of the play Helen is pregnant. She has undergone two deaths, one reported, one figurative, neither literal. And as she feared Bertram's literal death, she has brought about his figurative one instead. Bertram and Helen have died together.[8] The link with death may explain one of Shakespeare's changes from Boccaccio: in the source Giletta and her husband have several encounters; here there is only one. However often we have sex, we die only once.

Shortly after the bed-trick the gulling of Paroles comes to a climax when he too is threatened with death. The bed-trick took place in the dark; Paroles, blindfolded, wants to die in the light: "O Lord, sir, let me live, or let me see my death!" (4.3.312–13). The blindfold is removed, the trick is discovered, and his life goes on. The surprising resilience with which he emerges from his ordeal may suggest by analogy a hope for the future of Helen and Bertram. The fact that these three different characters have all gone into ordeals in the dark, all of which involve versions of death, indicates a generalizing quality in the play's action at this point. Bertram is gulled as Paroles is; Paroles emerges restored as Helen will be. It may be no accident that Paroles, pleading for life, echoes the Clown's all-purpose, generalizing catch phrase, "O Lord, sir." The ease with which Helen takes Diana's place may reflect the ease with which the Clown claims his answer fits every question: "as Tib's rush [ring] for Tom's forefinger . . . as the nail to his hole . . . as the pudding to his skin" (2.2.23–27). But as the Clown finds that his answer will not serve after all (2.2.55–56), all this generalizing—the plot patterning and figurative language that link different deaths, the bawdy jokes that work on the level at which one act of copulation is like another—leaves an unanswered question. What can be resolved at this level for this particular man, and this particular woman?

Helen generalizes:

> But O, strange men,
> That can such sweet use make of what they hate
> When saucy trusting of the cozened thoughts
> Defiles the pitchy night! So lust doth play
> With what it loathes for that which is away.
> (4.4.21–25)

It is as though when he made love what she thought of was his hate. Other critics have seen in this speech a suppression of her own presence,[9] even Helen's "feelings of damaged self-worth."[10] The generalizing here—she makes it a matter of what men do, what lust does, not explicitly a comment on Bertram— is self-protective. What the speech says about Bertram himself, and her encounter with him, is painful. In the last scene, addressing him directly, she will put a better face on it: "when I was like this maid, / I found you wondrous kind" (5.3.309–10). Even this tribute to him as a lover carries a rueful qualification. He was good in bed, because he thought she was someone else.

Married, pregnant, and restored to life after seeming death, Helen may seem to direct us, as we would expect in a comedy, toward the future. She has passed through two kinds of imaginary death to new life. But something of the death-marked quality of the play's opening scenes clings to her, and whatever sexual pleasure she may have found in the dark with Bertram it was bound up with personal pain. And there is another element of the bed-trick that, like her use of her father's medicine to cure the King, brings the past back. In the later scenes of *Hamlet* the Ghost, very much against revenge-ghost tradition, makes no final reappearance, and Hamlet is curiously silent on the subject of his father. But something of the old King survives when Hamlet uses his signet to bring about the deaths of Rosencrantz and Guildenstern. A similar token of the dead figures in *All's Well*: the ring Helen gets from Bertram in the dark and produces at the end to prove that she was the woman he bedded. By her own account, the ring

> downward hath descended in his house
> From son to son some four or five descents
> Since the first father wore it.
> (3.7.23–25)

He bears, according to the King, his father's face, and he wears his father's ring. His father is no longer named explicitly; once again the play is generalizing. But something of him is present in the bed-trick, and in the last scene where Helen claims her husband. Boccaccio's Count cherishes the ring "for a certaine vertue that he knew it had."[11] In Shakespeare its virtue is that it commemorates the dead.

The last movement of the play begins with Helen in the position occupied by the two lost fathers in 1.1: dead, mourned, and idealized. Even before the finale, the Countess and Lafeu recall her, fondly and admiringly (4.5.8–16). The King, unconsciously anticipating the importance of the rings that will figure in the denouement, opens the last scene by declaring, "We lost a jewel of her" (5.3.1). Lafeu says of Bertram:

> He lost a wife
> Whose beauty did astonish the survey
> Of richest eyes; whose words all ears took captive;
> Whose dear perfection hearts that scorned to serve
> Humbly called mistress.
> (5.3.15–19)

Once again everyone seems, if not literally, all in black.

But this is a comic finale, and life has to go on. The King, exercising his authority to direct the action, declares, "The time is fair again" and tells Bertram to forget the wrong he did to Helen: "All is whole. / Not one word more of the consumèd time" (5.3.36, 38–39). The future is represented by Lafeu's daughter Maudlin, Bertram's next wife. But a speech in which Bertram describes his past relations with Maudlin shifts into a speech about Helen "whom myself, / Since I have lost, have loved" (5.3.53–54), and the King draws out the theme at length, concluding, "She's good that's gone" (5.3.60). Both men, as they speak, are drawn back to the past, to thinking of the dead. The King makes another effort: "Be this sweet Helen's knell, and now forget her. / Send forth your amorous token for fair Maudlin" (5.3.67–68). But the token turns out to be Helen's ring, which she gave to Bertram in the dark, and Maudlin herself, much discussed in the first part of the scene, never appears. There are new and darker thoughts of Helen and her death: the King suspects Bertram of having her murdered, and the Countess cries, "Now justice on the doers!" (5.3.117–18, 153–54). Finally, as Gérard de Narbon returns in the medicine that cures the King, and the old Count returns in the ring that figures in the bed-trick, Helen returns in her own person, ushered by Diana: "Dead though she be, she feels her young one kick. / So there's my riddle: one that's dead is quick" (5.3.302–3). The sex-death pun appears one last time: she died, and so she is quick. The new life inside her holds promise for the future, but while Boccaccio's heroine has already given birth and appears with a pair of twin boys, Helen's child, like Maudlin, is a promise of the future that remains unseen.

The notorious if-clauses that hedge about the finale suggest that while the riddle is solved the personal relations are not quite. Helen once again offers to face death, literally or figuratively: "If it appear not plain, and prove untrue, / Deadly divorce step between me and you" (5.3.317–18). Given the near-impossibility of literal divorce in this period, she may be calling for the divorce of death; she may indeed mean literal divorce, on the other hand, which would be, like her first loss of him, a kind of death. In any case, she is prepared once again to face death, as she has faced death of various kinds all along. We expect a comedy to free itself from the past, and from death. Rosalind loses her preoccupation with her lost father when she gets involved with Orlando, and Old Adam, who represents the lost virtue of the past, slips out of the play as silently as Lear's Fool. Olivia forgets to mourn for her brother. But the reunion of the twins in *Twelfth Night* draws on memories of their father's death (5.1.242–48), and this is a clue as to where Shakespeare would go in what was likely his next comedy. Throughout *All's Well That Ends Well* characters are touched by death and drawn back into the past. Even the title, promising a comedy, has a shadow behind it. Susan Snyder's note on Helen's quotation of the title, "All's well that ends well; still the fine's the crown" (4.4.35), relates it to the Latin tag *Finis coronat opus*, but that in turn recalls the moment in *2 Henry VI* when Clifford, mortally wounded, proclaims, "*La fin couronne les oeuvres*," and dies (5.2.28). A satisfying comic finale can be called a good ending; so can a good death. This may help to account for the lack of comic ebullience that has made this play slow to win favor, and has kept it out of the inner circle of Shakespearean hits. As Robert Ornstein notes, "*All's Well* seems gray if not bleak, not because its viewpoint is jaded or disillusioned but because its chief characters do not delight us by their verve or humor or expansiveness of thought."[12] They are, one might say, a bit broody. Ornstein adds, however, that after all "it is not a very dark comedy."[13] Marjorie Garber, though not writing about *All's Well* in particular, gives a clue: "Shakespearean Comedy is about the initial avoidance or displacement of the idea of death, the cognition and recognition of one's own mortality— and then, crucially, the acceptance, even the affirmation, of that mortality."[14] Just as *All's Well* shows a surprising rapport between young and old in Helen's relations with the older generation, it shows a larger community than the new society created by marriage in traditional theories of comedy. It is a community that includes the living and the dead. The living begin by mourning the dead. As they move forward their thoughts are drawn back into the past, and new life is possible only through some kind of confrontation with death. The dead themselves return, involved in the affairs of the living. Or, in the words of a later poet:

> We die with the dying:
> See, they depart, and we go with them.
> We are born with the dead:
> See, they return, and bring us with them.
>   (T. S. Eliot, *Little Gidding*)

Except that this is Shakespeare, not T. S. Eliot; the communion of the living and the dead is not a matter of religious mysticism but an extension of the human community, of the ties people form with each other, which has always been the business of comedy.

Notes

1. All references to *All's Well That Ends Well* are to the Oxford edition, edited by Susan Snyder (Oxford: Oxford University Press, 1993). References to other Shakespeare plays are to *The Complete Works of Shakespeare*, ed. David Bevington, 4th ed. (New York: HarperCollins, 1992).

2. J. L. Styan, "The Opening of *All's Well That Ends Well*: A Performance Approach," *Entering the Maze: Shakespeare's Art of Beginning*, ed. Robert F. Willson, Jr. (New York: Peter Lang, 1995), 158.

3. See Alexander Welsh, "The Loss of Men and Getting of Children: 'All's Well That Ends Well' and 'Measure for Measure,'" *Modern Language Review* 73 (1978): 17–18; and Mary Beth Rose, "Where Are the Mothers in Shakespeare? Options for Gender Representation in the English Renaissance," *Shakespeare Quarterly* 42 (1991): 304.

4. According to Garrett A. Sullivan, Jr., there is a difference between the cause of her grief and the way the world reads that grief: "'Be this sweet Helen's knell, and now forget her': Forgetting, Memory, and Identity in *All's Well That Ends Well*," *Shakespeare Quarterly* 50 (1999): 52.

5. See ibid., 60.

6. Robertson Davies, in an essay designed to deflect some of the criticism to which Bertram has long been subject, writes, "Bertram's conduct with Diana hardly seems to call for comment. So long as armies serve abroad such stories will be told": Tyrone Guthrie, Robertson Davies, and Grant MacDonald, *Renown at Stratford* (Toronto: Clarke, Irwin and Company, 1953), 74–75.

7. See Kate Aughterson, ed., *Renaissance Woman: Constructions of Femininity in England* (London and New York: Routledge, 1995), 43, 57–60.

8. According to David McCandless, the report of Helen's literal death "becomes the only means of registering the metaphorical death she experiences during the bed-trick, the only means of invoking her sexual pleasure": "Helena's Bed-trick: Gender and Performance in *All's Well That Ends Well*," *Shakespeare Quarterly* 45 (1994): 462.

9. Barbara Hodgdon, "The Making of Virgins and Mothers: Sexual Signs, Substitute Scenes and Doubled Presences in *All's Well That Ends Well*," *Philological Quarterly* 66 (1987): 61.

10. R. B. Parker, "War and Sex in 'All's Well that Ends Well,'" *Shakespeare Survey* 37 (1984): 111.

11. Geoffrey Bullough, ed., *Narrative and Dramatic Sources of Shakespeare*, vol. 2 (London: Routledge and Kegan Paul; New York: Columbia University Press, 1968), 392.

12. Robert Ornstein, *Shakespeare's Comedies: From Roman Farce to Romantic Mystery* (Newark: University of Delaware Press, 1986), 173.

13. Ibid., 194.

14. Marjorie Garber, "'Wild Laughter in the Throat of Death': Darker Purposes in Shakespearean Comedy," in *Shakespearean Comedy*, ed. Maurice Charney (New York: New York Literary Forum, 1980), 121. Oddly, the article makes only one passing reference to *All's Well*, expressing dissatisfaction with its ending, 123.

Chronology

1564	William Shakespeare christened at Stratford-on-Avon on April 26.
1582	Marries Anne Hathaway in November.
1583	Daughter Susanna born, baptized on May 26.
1585	Twins, Hamnet and Judith, are born, baptized on February 2.
1587	Shakespeare goes to London, without family.
1589–90	*Henry VI, Part 1* written.
1590–91	*Henry VI, Part 2* and *Henry VI, Part 3* written.
1592–93	*Richard III* and *The Two Gentlemen of Verona* written.
1593	Publication of *Venus and Adonis*, dedicated to the Earl of Southampton; the sonnets probably begun.
1593	*The Comedy of Errors* written.
1593–94	Publication of *The Rape of Lucrece*, also dedicated to the Earl of Southampton. *Titus Andronicus* and *The Taming of the Shrew* written.
1594–95	*Love's Labour's Lost*, *King John*, and *Richard II* written.
1595–96	*Romeo and Juliet* and *A Midsummer Night's Dream* written.
1596	Son, Hamnet, dies.

1596–97	*The Merchant of Venice* and *Henry IV, Part 1* written; purchases New Place in Stratford.
1597–98	*The Merry Wives of Windsor* and *Henry IV, Part 2* written.
1598–99	*Much Ado about Nothing* written.
1599	*Henry V, Julius Caesar*, and *As You Like It* written.
1600–01	*Hamlet* written.
1601	*The Phoenix and the Turtle* written; father dies.
1601–02	*Twelfth Night* and *Troilus and Cressida* written.
1602–03	*All's Well That Ends Well* written.
1603	Shakespeare's company becomes the King's Men.
1604	*Measure for Measure* and *Othello* written.
1605	*King Lear* written.
1606	*Macbeth* and *Antony and Cleopatra* written.
1607	Marriage of daughter Susanna on June 5.
1607–08	*Coriolanus, Timon of Athens*, and *Pericles* written.
1608	Mother dies.
1609	Publication, probably unauthorized, of the quarto edition of the *Sonnets*.
1609–10	*Cymbeline* written.
1610–11	*The Winter's Tale* written.
1611	*The Tempest* written. Shakespeare returns to Stratford, where he will live until his death.
1612	*A Funeral Elegy* written.
1612–13	*Henry VIII* written; the Globe Theatre destroyed by fire.
1613	*The Two Noble Kinsmen* written (with John Fletcher).
1616	Daughter Judith marries on February 10; Shakespeare dies April 23.
1623	Publication of the First Folio edition of Shakespeare's plays.

Contributors

HAROLD BLOOM is Sterling Professor of the Humanities at Yale University. Educated at Cornell and Yale universities, he is the author of more than 30 books, including *Shelley's Mythmaking* (1959), *The Visionary Company* (1961), *Blake's Apocalypse* (1963), *Yeats* (1970), *The Anxiety of Influence* (1973), *A Map of Misreading* (1975), *Kabbalah and Criticism* (1975), *Agon: Toward a Theory of Revisionism* (1982), *The American Religion* (1992), *The Western Canon* (1994), *Omens of Millennium: The Gnosis of Angels, Dreams, and Resurrection* (1996), *Shakespeare: The Invention of the Human* (1998), *How to Read and Why* (2000), *Genius: A Mosaic of One Hundred Exemplary Creative Minds* (2002), *Hamlet: Poem Unlimited* (2003), *Where Shall Wisdom Be Found?* (2004), and *Jesus and Yahweh: The Names Divine* (2005). In addition, he is the author of hundreds of articles, reviews, and editorial introductions. In 1999, Professor Bloom received the American Academy of Arts and Letters' Gold Medal for Criticism. He has also received the International Prize of Catalonia, the Alfonso Reyes Prize of Mexico, and the Hans Christian Andersen Bicentennial Prize of Denmark.

NORTHROP FRYE was university professor at the University of Toronto and also a professor of English in Victoria College at the University of Toronto for many years. He wrote numerous books, including the seminal work *Anatomy of Criticism*.

RUTH NEVO is a professor emeritus of the Hebrew University of Jerusalem. She is the author of *Comic Transformation in Shakespeare* and *Shakespeare's Other Language*.

RENÉ GIRARD is emeritus professor at Stanford University. He authored numerous works, including *A Theater of Envy: William Shakespeare,* and *Violence and the Sacred.*

ARTHUR KIRSCH is a professor of English, emeritus, University of Virginia. He has written extensively on Shakespeare as well as on Auden and has edited a new edition of Auden's *The Sea and the Mirror: A Commentary on Shakespeare's "The Tempest."*

ALAN STEWART is a professor of English and comparative literature at Columbia University. His published work includes *Shakespeare's Letters,* and he has edited *Henry VI, Parts 1, 2,* and *3.*

W.H. AUDEN was a poet, essayist, playwright, editor, and librettist. He was Professor of Poetry at the University of Oxford and taught at several universities in the United States. He wrote many volumes of poetry and edited or coedited many anthologies, including *Poets of the English Language.*

RICHARD HARP is a professor of English at the University of Nevada–Las Vegas, where he also is department chairman. He has published on Shakespeare, with his books including work on Ben Jonson as well as *Dr. Johnson's Critical Vocabulary.* He is the founding coeditor of *The Ben Jonson Journal.*

ALEXANDER LEGGATT has been a professor of English at University College, University of Toronto. He has published several titles on Shakespeare's works, including *Shakespeare's Comedy of Love.* He also is the editor of *The Cambridge Companion to Shakespearean Comedy* and other titles.

Bibliography

Alvis, John E., and Thomas G. West, ed. *Shakespeare as Political Thinker*. Wilmington, Del.: ISI Books, 2000.

Auden, W. H. *The Sea and the Mirror: A Commentary on Shakespeare's* The Tempest, edited by Arthur Kirsch. Princeton, N.J.: Princeton University Press, 2003.

Bate, Jonathan, ed. *Shakespeare and the Twentieth Century*. Newark, Del.; London, England: University of Delaware Press; Associated University Presses, 1998.

Berger, Harry, Jr. *Making Trifles of Terror*. Stanford, Calif.: Stanford University Press, 1997.

Bielmeier, Michael G. *Shakespeare, Kierkegaard, and Existential Tragedy*. Lewiston, N.Y.: Edwin Mellon Press, 2000.

Bloom, Allan. *Shakespeare on Love and Friendship*. Chicago: University of Chicago Press, 2000.

Bowen, Barbara E. *Gender in the Theater of War: Shakespeare's* Troilus and Cressida. New York: Garland, 1993.

Charnes, Linda. *Notorious Identity: Materializing the Subject in Shakespeare*. Cambridge, Mass.: Harvard University Press, 1993.

Charney, Maurice. *Wrinkled Deep in Time: Aging in Shakespeare*. New York: Columbia University Press, 2009.

Clark, Ira. *Rhetorical Readings, Dark Comedies, and Shakespeare's Problem Plays*. Gainesville: University Press of Florida, 2007.

Cohen, Stephen, ed. *Shakespeare and Historical Formalism*. Aldershot, England; Burlington, Vt.: Ashgate, 2007.

Crider, Scott F. *With What Persuasion: An Essay on Shakespeare and the Ethics of Rhetoric*. New York: Peter Lang, 2009.

Crosman, Robert. *The World's a Stage: Shakespeare and the Dramatic View of Life.* Bethesda: Academica Press, 2005.

Dutton, Richard, and Jean E. Howard, ed. *A Companion to Shakespeare's Works.* Malden, Mass.: Blackwell, 2003.

Fawkner, H. W. *Shakespeare's Miracle Plays:* Pericles, Cymbeline, *and* The Winter's Tale. Rutherford, N.J.: Fairleigh Dickinson University Press; London: Associated University Presses, 1992.

Garber, Marjorie. *Shakespeare and Modern Culture.* New York: Pantheon, 2008.

Graff, Gerald, and James Phelan, ed. *William Shakespeare:* The Tempest: *A Case Study in Critical Controversy.* Boston, Mass.: Bedford, 2000.

Haley, David. *Shakespeare's Courtly Mirror: Reflexivity and Prudence in* All's Well That Ends Well. Newark: University of Delaware Press; London; Cranbury, N.J.: Associated University Presses, 1993.

Harmon, A. G. *Eternal Bonds, True Contracts: Law and Nature in Shakespeare's Problem Plays.* Albany: State University of New York Press, 2004.

Hunt, Maurice. *Shakespeare's Romance of the Word.* Lewisburg: Bucknell University Press, 1990.

Jordan, Constance. *Shakespeare's Monarchies: Ruler and Subject in the Romances.* Ithaca, N.Y.: Cornell University Press, 1997.

Lamb, Mary Ellen, and Valerie Wayne, ed. *Staging Early Modern Romance: Prose Fiction, Dramatic Romance, and Shakespeare.* New York: Routledge, 2009.

Levin, Harry. *Scenes from Shakespeare.* New York: Garland, 2000.

Levin, Richard. *Looking for an Argument: Critical Encounters with the New Approaches to the Criticism of Shakespeare and His Contemporaries.* Madison, N.J.; London, England: Fairleigh Dickinson University Press; Associated University Presses, 2003.

Maguire, Laurie, ed. *How to Do Things with Shakespeare: New Approaches, New Essays.* Malden, Mass.: Blackwell, 2008.

McCandless, David. *Gender and Performance in Shakespeare's Problem Comedies.* Bloomington: Indiana University Press, 1997.

Meek, Richard. *Narrating the Visual in Shakespeare.* Farnham, England; Burlington, Vt.: Ashgate, 2009.

Montrose, Louis. *The Purpose of Playing: Shakespeare and the Cultural Politics of the Elizabethan Theatre.* Chicago: University of Chicago Press, 1996.

Murley, John A., and Sean D. Sutton, ed. *Perspectives on Politics in Shakespeare.* Lanham, Md.: Lexington Books, 2006.

Olson, Paul A. *Beyond a Common Joy: An Introduction to Shakespearean Comedy.* Lincoln: University of Nebraska Press, 2008.

Orlin, Lena Cowen, and Miranda Johnson-Haddad, ed. *Staging Shakespeare: Essays in Honor of Alan C. Dessen.* Newark: University of Delaware Press, 2007.

Porterfield, Sally F. *Jung's Advice to the Players: A Jungian Reading of Shakespeare's Problem Plays.* Westport, Conn.: Greenwood Press, 1994.

Redmond, Michael J. *Shakespeare, Politics, and Italy: Intertextuality on the Jacobean Stage.* Farnham, England; Burlington, Vt.: Ashgate, 2009.

Richards, Jennifer, and James Knowles, ed. *Shakespeare's Late Plays: New Readings.* Edinburgh: Edinburgh University Press, 1999.

Rist, Thomas. *Shakespeare's Romances and the Politics of Counter-Reformation.* Lewiston, N.Y.: Mellen, 1999.

Shannon, Laurie. *Sovereign Amity: Figures of Friendship in Shakespearean Contexts.* Chicago: University of Chicago Press, 2002.

Smith, Stephen W., and Travis Curtright, ed. *Shakespeare's Last Plays: Essays in Literature and Politics.* Lanham, Md.: Lexington, 2002.

Snyder, Susan. *Shakespeare: A Wayward Journey.* Newark, Del.; London, England: University of Delaware Press; Associated University Presses, 2002.

Stagman, Myron. *Shakespeare's Double-Dealing Comedies: Deciphering the Problem Plays.* Newcastle: Cambridge Scholars, 2010.

Thomas, Vivian. *The Moral Universe of Shakespeare's Problem Plays.* Totowa, N.J.: Barnes & Noble Books, 1987.

Thorne, Alison, ed. *Shakespeare's Romances.* Houndmills, Basingstoke, Hampshire; New York: Palgrave Macmillan, 2003.

Tucker, Kenneth. *Shakespeare and Jungian Typology: A Reading of the Plays.* Jefferson, N.C.: McFarland & Co., 2003.

Weitz, Morris. *Shakespeare, Philosophy, and Literature: Essays.* New York, N.Y.: Peter Lang, 1995.

Wells, Stanley, ed. *Shakespeare in the Theatre: An Anthology of Criticism.* Oxford, England: Clarendon, 1997.

Wells, Stanley, and Lena Cowen Orlin, ed. *Shakespeare: An Oxford Guide.* New York: Oxford University Press, 2003.

Yachnin, Paul, and Patricia Badir, ed. *Shakespeare and the Cultures of Performance.* Aldershot, England; Burlington, Vt.: Ashgate, 2008.

Acknowledgments

Northrop Frye, "Shakespeare's Romances: *The Winter's Tale.*" From *Northrop Frye on Shakespeare*, edited by Robert Sandler. Published by Yale University Press (U.S.) and Fitzhenry and Whiteside (Canada). Copyright © 1986 by Northrop Frye.

Ruth Nevo, "*Cymbeline*: The Rescue of the King." From *Shakespeare's Other Language*. Published by Methuen. Copyright © 1987 by Ruth Nevo.

René Girard, "The Crime and Conversion of Leontes in *The Winter's Tale.*" From *Religion and Literature* 22, nos. 2–3 (Summer–Autumn 1990): 193–219. Copyright © 1990 by the Department of English, University of Notre Dame.

Arthur Kirsch, "Virtue, Vice, and Compassion in Montaigne and *The Tempest.*" From *Studies in English Literature, 1500–1900* 37, no. 2 (Spring 1997): 337–52. Copyright © 1997 by Rice University.

Alan Stewart, "'Near Akin': The Trials of Friendship in *The Two Noble Kinsmen.*" From *Shakespeare's Late Plays: New Readings*, edited by Jennifer Richards and James Knowles. Copyright © 1999 by Edinburgh University Press.

W.H. Auden, "*Troilus and Cressida.*" From *Lectures on Shakespeare*, reconstructed and edited by Arthur Kirsch. Copyright © 2000 by Arthur Kirsch for the notes and © 2000 by the estate of W. H. Auden for lectures and writings by Auden.

Richard Harp. "The Consolation of Romance: Providence in Shakespeare's Late Plays." From *Shakespeare's Last Plays: Essays in Literature and Politics*, edited by Stephen W. Smith and Travis Curtright. Copyright © 2002 by Lexington Books.

Alexander Leggatt, "In the Shadow of *Hamlet*: Comedy and Death in *All's Well That Ends Well*." From *Re-Visions of Shakespeare: Essays in Honor of Robert Ornstein*, edited by Evelyn Gajowksi. Published by University of Delaware Press. Copyright © 2004 by Rosemont Publishing and Printing

Index

Characters in literary works are listed by first name followed by the work in which they appear.